Illinois Bicycle Trails

An American Bike Trails Publication

Illinois Bicycle Trails

Published by American Bike Trails
Copyright 2010 by American Bike Trails

Created by   Ray Hoven
Illustrated & Designed by   Mary C. Rumpsa

Table of Contents

Table of Contents (continued)

Table of Contents (continued)

How To Use This Book

This book provides a comprehensive, easy-to-use quick reference to most of the off-road bicycle trails throughout Illinois. It contains over 160 trails with some 130 of those illustrated with detail maps, plus overviews covering the state by section and selective counties. Illustrated and non-illustrated maps are generally shown alphabetically. The back of the book contains a listing of selected parks in the state with pertinent information on each, plus a trail listing in alphabetical sequence, a cross-reference by city to trail and by county to trail. Each trail map includes such helpful features as trail statistics, location and access, trail facilities, and nearby communities.

Terms Used

Length
: Expressed in miles. Round trip mileage is normally indicated for loops.

Effort Levels
: **Easy** Physical exertion is not strenuous. Climbs and descents as well as technical obstacles are more minimal. Recommended for beginners.

: **Moderate** Physical exertion is not excessive. Climbs and descents can be challenging. Expect some technical obstacles.

: **Difficult** Physical exertion is demanding. Climbs and descents require good riding skills. Trail surface may be sandy, loose rock, soft or wet.

Directions
: Describes by way of directions and distances, how to get to the trail areas from roads and nearby communities.

Map
: Illustrative representation of a geographic area, such as a state, section, forest, park or trail complex.

Forest
: Typically encompasses a dense growth of trees and underbrush covering a large tract.

Park
: A tract of land generally including woodlands and open areas.

DNR
: Department of Natural Resources

Types of Biking

Mountain   Fat-tired bikes are recommended. Ride may be generally flat but then with a soft, rocky or wet surface.

Leisure   Off-road gentle ride. Surface is generally paved or screened.

Riding Tips

Pushing in gears that are too high can push knees beyond their limits. Avoid extremes by pedaling faster rather than shifting into a higher gear.

Keeping your elbows bent, changing your hand position frequently and wearing bicycle gloves all help to reduce the numbness or pain in the palm of the hand from long-distance riding.

Keep you pedal rpms up on an uphill so you have reserve power if you lose speed.

Stay in a high-gear on a level surface, placing pressure on the pedals and resting on the handle bars and saddle.

Lower your center of gravity on a long or steep downhill run by using the quick release seat post binder and dropping the saddle height down.

Brake intermittently on a rough surface.

Wear proper equipment. Wear a helmet that is approved by the Snell Memorial Foundation or the American National Standards Institute. Look for one of their stickers inside the helmet.

Use a lower tire inflation pressure for riding on unpaved surfaces. The lower pressure will provide better tire traction and a more comfortable ride.

Apply your brakes gradually to maintain control on loose gravel or soil.

Ride only on trails designated for bicycles or in areas where you have the permission of the landowner.

Be courteous to hikers or horseback riders on the trail, they have the right of way.

Leave riding trails in the condition you found them. Be sensitive to the environment. Properly dispose of your trash. If you open a gate, close it behind you.

Don't carry items or attach anything to your bicycle that might hinder your vision or control.

Don't wear anything that restricts your hearing.

Don't carry extra clothing where it can hang down and jam in a wheel.

Explanation of Symbols

TRAIL USES

- Bicycling
- Mountain Bicycling
- Hiking
- Cross-Country Skiing
- Inline Skating
- Snowmobiling
- Bridal Path

FACILITIES

- Beach/Swimming
- Bicycle Repair
- Cabin
- Camping
- Canoe Launch
- First Aid
- Food
- Golf Course
- Information
- Lodging
- Multi-Facilities
- Parking
- Picnic
- Ranger Station
- Restrooms
- Shelter
- Trailhead
- Visitor/Nature Center
- Water
- Overlook/Observation

MAP SYMBOLS

- State Line
- County Line
- Bridge/Tunnel
- City
- Park
- Waterway
- Interstate Route
- US Route
- State Road
- County Road
- Exit Number
- Airport
- Point of Interest

TRAIL SYMBOLS

- Biking Trail
- Bike Route/Lane
- Alternate Trail
- Planned Trail
- Railroad Tracks

Health Hazards

Hypothermia

Hypothermia is a condition where the core body temperature falls below 90 degrees. This may cause death.

Mild hypothermia

1. **Symptoms**

    a. Pronounced shivering

    b. Loss of physical coordination

    c. Thinking becomes cloudy

2. **Causes**

    a. Cold, wet, loss of body heat, wind

3. **Treatment**

    a. Prevent further heat loss, get out of wet clothing and out of wind. Replace wet clothing with dry.

    b. Help body generate more heat. Refuel with high-energy foods and a hot drink, get moving around, light exercise, or external heat.

Severe hypothermia

1. **Symptoms**

    a. Shivering stops, pulse and respiration slows down, speech becomes incoherent.

2. **Treatment**

    a. Get help immediately.

    b. Don't give food or water.

    c. Don't try to re-warm the victim in the field.

d. A buildup of toxic wastes and tactic acid accumulates in the blood in the body's extremities. Movement or rough handling will cause a flow of the blood from the extremities to the heart. This polluted blood can send the heart into ventricular fibrillations (heart attack). This may result in death.

e. Wrap victim in several sleeping bags and insulate from the ground.

Frostbite

Symptoms of frostbite may include red skin with white blotches due to lack of circulation. Re-warm body parts gently. Do not immerse in hot water or rub to restore circulation, as both will destroy skin cells.

Heat Exhaustion

Cool, pale, and moist skin, heavy sweating, headache, nausea, dizziness and vomiting. Body temperature nearly normal.

Treatment

Have victim lie in the coolest place available – on back with feet raised. Rub body gently with cool, wet cloth. Give person ½ glass of water every 15 minutes if conscious and can tolerate it. Call for emergency medical assistance.

Heat Stroke

Hot, red skin, shock or unconsciousness; high body temperature.

Treatment

Treat as a life-threatening emergency. Call for emergency medical assistance immediately. Cool victim by any means possible. Cool bath, pour cool water over body, or wrap wet sheets around body. Give nothing by mouth.

State of Illinois

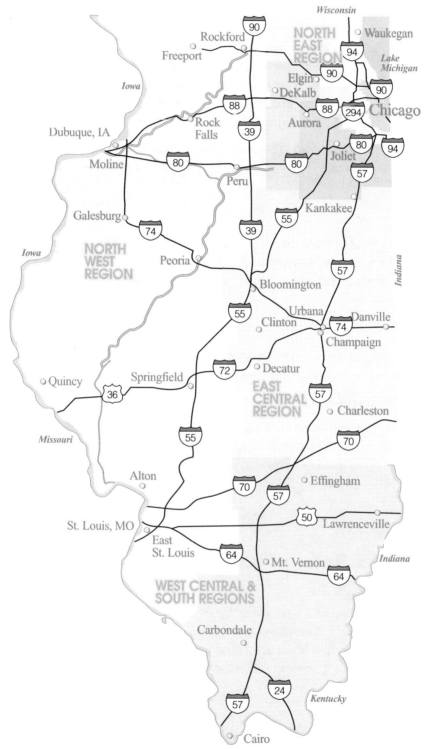

Mileage Between Principal Cities

CITY	SPRINGFIELD	ST. LOUIS, MO	ROCKFORD	PEORIA	CHICAGO	CHAMPAIGN
BLOOMINGTON	64	163	136	40	136	53
CAIRO	242	148	426	312	375	244
CARBONDALE	172	108	384	242	333	202
CHAMPAIGN	86	182	188	92	137	
CHICAGO	201	300	83	170		137
DECATUR	39	118	179	83	178	47
DE KALB	183	282	44	124	66	174
DUBUQUE, IA	238	337	91	167	176	259
EFFINGHAM	89	104	260	164	209	78
ELGIN	208	307	48	148	37	169
GALESBURG	120	219	150	49	198	141
KANKAKEE	158	254	138	121	56	78
LAWRENCEVILLE	154	147	309	213	250	127
MOLINE	163	262	117	92	165	184
MT. VERNON	146	82	330	216	279	148
PEORIA	71	170	138		170	92
QUINCY	110	133	269	131	310	195
ROCKFORD	197	296		138	83	188
ST. LOUIS, MO	100		296	170	300	182
SPRINGFIELD		100	197	71	201	86
WAUKEGAN	229	328	71	198	40	181

North West Region

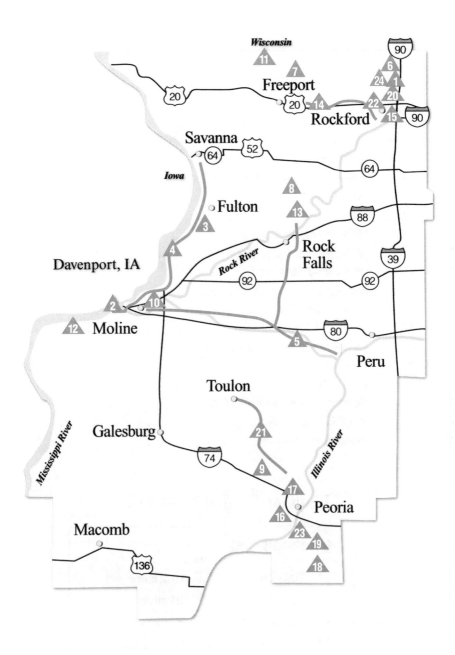

Wisconsin

Freeport

Rockford

Savanna

Iowa

Fulton

Rock Falls

Davenport, IA

Rock River

Moline

Peru

Toulon

Galesburg

Illinois River

Peoria

Macomb

Mississippi River

20 20 20 14 11 7 6 24 1 22 20 15 90 64 52 64 8 13 88 39 3 4 92 92 2 10 12 5 80 21 9 74 17 16 23 19 18 136

North East Region

Planning for that Trail Visit

Checkoff List
Information you may want to have at hand

- ☐ Trail location
- ☐ Trail accesses
- ☐ Parking
- ☐ Restrooms
- ☐ Drinking water
- ☐ Refreshments
- ☐ Lodging
- ☐ Conditions

- ☐ Local area events
- ☐ Telephone access
- ☐ Bicycle service
- ☐ Picnic facilities
- ☐ Shelters
- ☐ Camping facilities
- ☐ Emergency assistance phone number

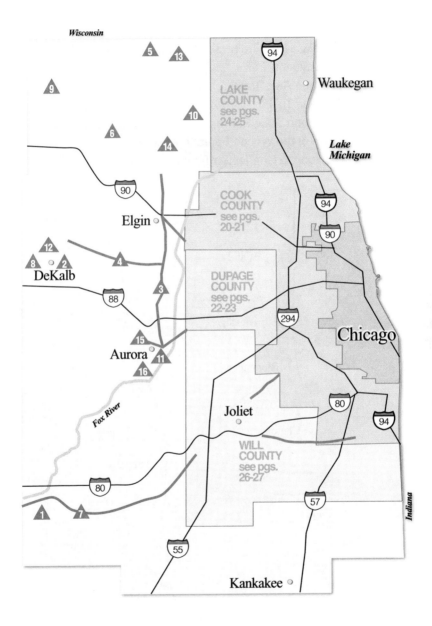

Wisconsin

5　13

9

10

LAKE
COUNTY
see pgs.
24-25

94

Waukegan

Lake
Michigan

6

14

90

Elgin

COOK
COUNTY
see pgs.
20-21

94

90

12

8　2

4

DeKalb

3

88

DUPAGE
COUNTY
see pgs.
22-23

294

Chicago

15

Aurora　11

16

80

94

Fox River

Joliet

WILL
COUNTY
see pgs.
26-27

80

1　7

80

57

Indiana

55

Kankakee

East Central Region

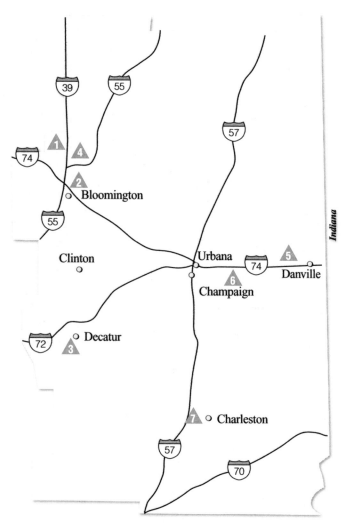

West Central & South Regions

Cook County

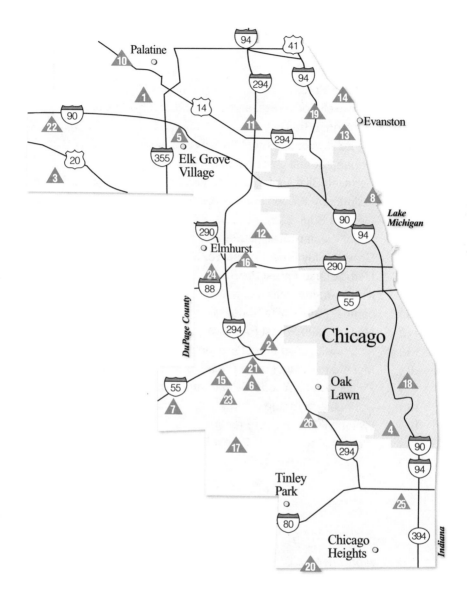

DuPage County

Bicycle Resources

Bicycling Brochure (Free)

Illinois Department of Conservation
Office of Resource Marketing and Education
524 South Second Street
Springfield, IL 62701-1787

(217) 782-7454

Information brochure listing off-road bicycle trails statewide. The Department of Conservation also distributes an attractive Illinois State Parks magazine as well as brochures on hiking, camping, and other outdoor activities.

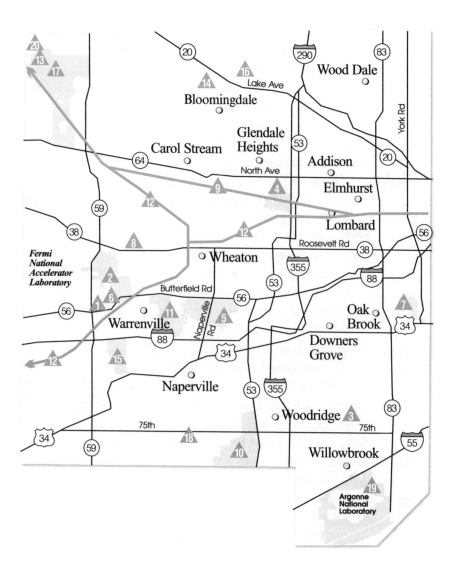

Wood Dale

Bloomingdale

Lake Ave

Glendale
Heights

Carol Stream

North Ave

Addison

Elmhurst

York Rd

Fermi
National
Accelerator
Laboratory

Wheaton

Lombard

Roosevelt Rd

Butterfield Rd

Warrenville

Naperville Rd

Oak
Brook

Downers
Grove

Naperville

Woodridge

75th

75th

Willowbrook

Argonne
National
Laboratory

Lake County

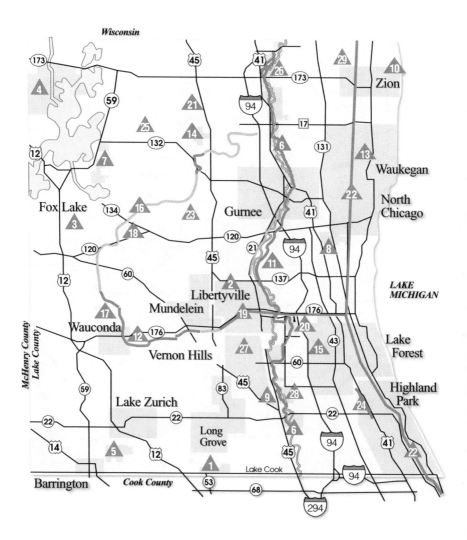

Bicycle Maintenance Checklist

Inspect your bicycle for the following:

Tires should not have cracks on the sidewalls, cuts in the tread or excessive wear. Using proper tire pressure, printed on the sidewall of the tire, prevents excessive wear.

Gear and brake cables move freely. Replace rusted or frayed cables.

The chain should be free of rust. Too much oil will attract dust and dirt, shortening the life of the chain.

Pedals are securely fastened, and pedal reflectors are clean and visible.

This checklist takes only a few minutes and may prevent you from having an accident or mechanical breakdown.

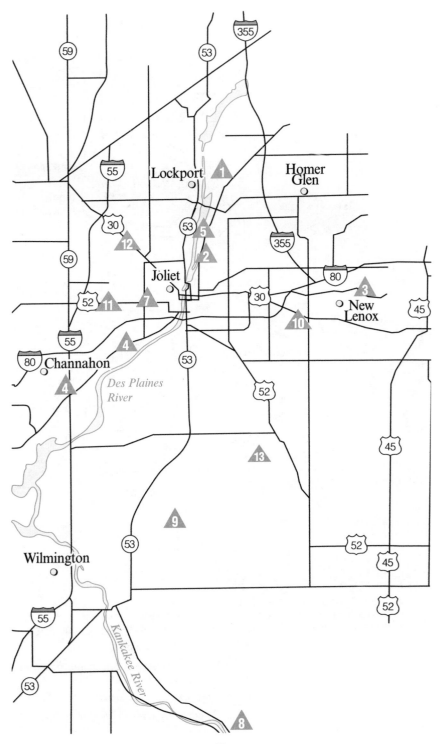

Will County

Wauponsee Glacial Trail

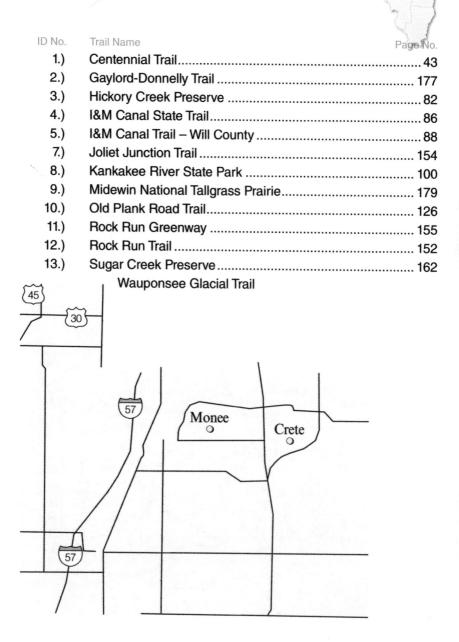

Madison County Trails

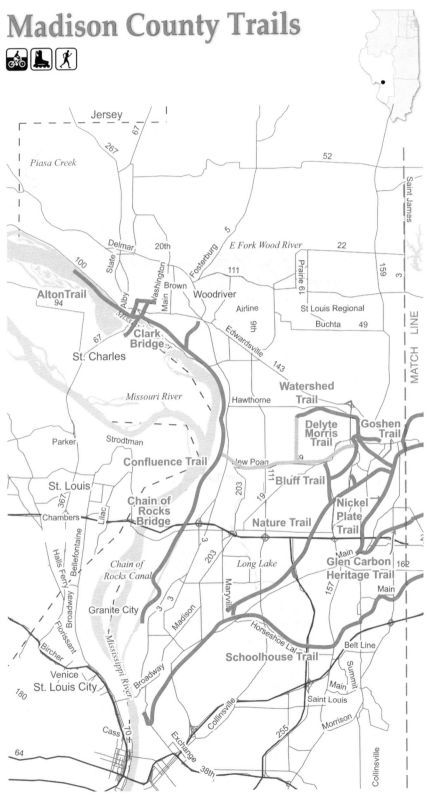

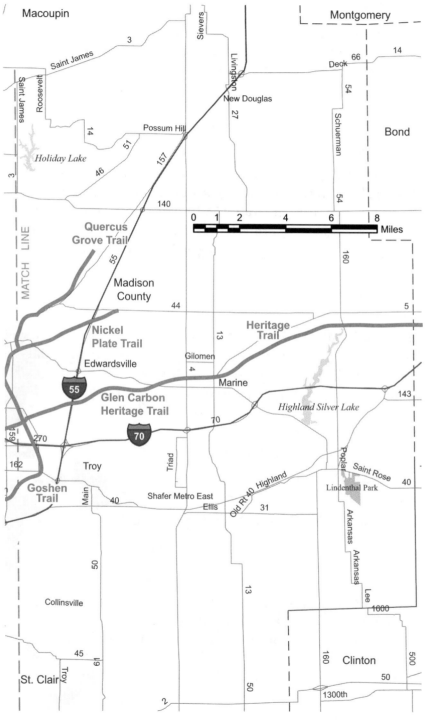

Macoupin

Montgomery

Saint James

Sievers

Livingston

3

Deck 66

14

Roosevelt

Saint James

New Douglas

54

Schuerman

Bond

Saint James

14

51

Possum Hill

27

157

Holiday Lake

46

3

140

MATCH LINE

0 1 2   4   6   8
Miles

Quercus
Grove Trail

55

160

Madison
County

44

5

Nickel
Plate Trail

13

Heritage
Trail

Gilomen

Edwardsville

4

Marine

55

Glen Carbon
Heritage Trail

Highland Silver Lake

143

70

70

159

270

Triad

Poplar

Saint Rose

40

162

Troy

Highland

Lindenthal Park

Goshen
Trail

Main

40

Shafer Metro East

Old Rt 40

Ellis

31

Arkansas

Arkansas

00

13

Lee

1600

Collinsville

160

Clinton

500

45

Troy

50

St. Clair

50

2

1300th

Alton Trail

Trail Length 4 miles   **Surface** Asphalt

Location & Setting This trail extends along the Mississippi River from the Clark Bridge through Alton parks. There are connections to Clark Bridge, Confluence Trail, and the Vadalabene Great River Road Trail.

Information   Alton Parks & Recreation   (818) 463-3580

Bluff Trail

Trail Length 2 miles   **Surface** Asphalt

Location & Setting Located in Edwardsville, this trail travels alongside the ancient bluffs and prairie grass restoration areas of the Great American Bottoms. Parking is available on Bluff Road at the So. Illinois University Extension (SIUE), Delyte Morris Trail, Korte Stadium and at St. Paul's Church of Christ in Edwardsville.

Information   Madison County Transit Trails   (618) 874-7433

Chain of Rocks Bridge

Trail Length 1 mile   **Surface** Concrete

Location & Setting Connects Granite City to Riverview, Missouri. This bridge provides one of three bicycle-accessible connections between Illinois and Missouri by linking the St. Louis Riverfront and the Confluence Trail.

Information   Trailnet (314) 416-9930

Clark Bridge

Trail Length 1 mile   **Surface** Asphalt

Location & Setting Connects Alton, Illinois to West Alton, Missouri. This bike lane links the Alton and Confluence Trail to the West Alton Trail.

Information   Illinois Dept. of Transportation   (618) 346-3100

Confluence Trail

Trail Length 18.6 miles **Surface** Asphalt, oil & chip

Location & Setting Connects Alton to Granite City, and provides spectacular views of the Mississippi River, a 900-foot bridge over Wood River Creek, popular stops such as the Lock & Dam 26 Visitor's Center in East Alton, and the Lewis & Clark Interpretive Center in Hartford. Parking is also available at Russell Commons Park in Alton, and at both the IL and MO side of the Chain of Rock Bridge.

Information   Madison County Transit Trails   (618) 874-7433

Delyte Morris Trail

Trail Length 2.5 miles   **Surface** Asphalt

Location & Setting This path proceeds from the courthouse in Edwardsville to Bluff Road on the western edge of the SIUE campus. From Edwardsville the trail continues down a small valley and through some heavily wooded area. Sections are rugged with hilly terrain. Parking is available at the Cougar Lake Recreation Area.

Information   SIUE Campus Recreation Office   (619) 650-2348

Glen Carbon Heritage Trail

Trail Length 11 miles   **Surface** Asphalt and crushed stone

Location & Setting The trail follows the old Illinois Central RR route from Hwy 255, through Glen Carbon, a natural passage in the bluffs, and onto restored prairies on top of the bluffs. Parking, restroom and picnic facilities can be found in Miner Park, a few blocks off the trail in Glen Carbon. Along the trail are several historical markers and 7 timber trestle bridges. The Silver Creek Railroad trestle is 340 feet long. A suggested trail starting off point is from behind the fire station in Glen Carbon or from Miner Park.

Information   Madison County Transit Trails   (618) 874-7433

Goshen Trail

Trail Length 7.0 miles   **Surface** Asphalt

Location & Setting The trail runs between Troy & Edwardsville. It connects to the Schoolhouse, Heritage, Nature, Delyte Morris, Watershed, and Nickel Plate trails, and provides access to neighborhoods throughout the county with 10 tunnels & a 175-foot bridge.

Information   Madison County Transit Trails   (618) 874-7433

Heritage Trail

Trail Length 12.8 miles   **Surface** Crushed limestone, asphalt

Location & Setting This trail runs from Glen Carbon to Marine. It passes endless fields, nearby Citizen and Miner Park, and connects to Marine Village Park, Goshen Trail and Nickel Plate Trail.

Information   Village of Glen Carbon   (618) 288-1200

Madison County Trails (continued)

Nature Trail

Trail Length 12.7 miles   **Surface** Asphalt

Location & Setting The Nature Trail runs from Edwardsville to Granite City. Expect to see an abundance of wildlife on this wooded path and it spans creeks and connect to neighborhoods, schools and parks. Parking is available at Longfellow & Nelson Avenues, Edwardsville High School during non-school hours, and the Park and Bike lot on Revelle Lane in Pontoon Beach.

Information   Madison County Transit Trails   (618) 874-7433

Nickel Plate Trail

Trail Length 13.7 miles   **Surface** Asphalt

Location & Setting Fruit Rd in Edwardsville to Old Edwardsville Rd in Pontoon Beach. The setting features a combination of woods and farmland, with access to parks, neighborhoods, and historic districts in Edwardsville and Glen Carbon. Parking is available at Longfellow Rd at Nelson Ave, at Longfellow Rd at Hwy 159, and at Main Street in Glen Carbon behind the ball field.

Information   Madison County Transit Trails   (618) 874-7433

Quercus Grove Trail

Trail Length 5.8 miles   **Surface** Asphalt, limestone screenings

Location & Setting The trail connects historic downtown Edwardsville with miles of serene fields. Parking is available in Edwardsville at the Park and Ride Lot for the Madison County Transit Edwardsville Station.

Information   Madison County Transit Trails   (618) 874-7433

Schoolhouse Trail

Trail Length 15.9 miles   **Surface** Asphalt

Location & Setting The Schoolhouse Trail runs from Troy to Madison. The ride features fields, Horseshoe Lake State Park, Gateway Center, Splash City Water Park, and Drost Park. Parking is available at Horseshoe Lake State Park, the Gateway Convention Center in Collinsville, at Drost Park in Mayville, and at Hwy 162 at Edwardsville/Troy Rd in Troy.

Information   Madison County Transit Trails   (618) 874-7433

Watershed Trail

Trail Length 4.7 miles   **Surface** Asphalt

Location & Setting The Watershed Trail is built along abandoned rail corridor between West Union Street in Edwardsville and northwest to the Watershed Nature Center and Wanda Rd in Roxana. The ride over vintage railroad trestles offers dramatic views of historic Cahokia Creek. There is parking on Russell Rd and at the Watershed Nature Center on Tower Ave adjacent to the N.O. Nelson Elementary School in Edwardsville.

Information   Madison County Transit Trails   (618) 874-7433

Rockford Area

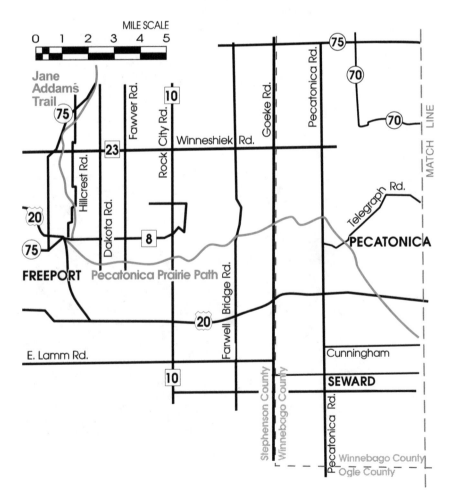

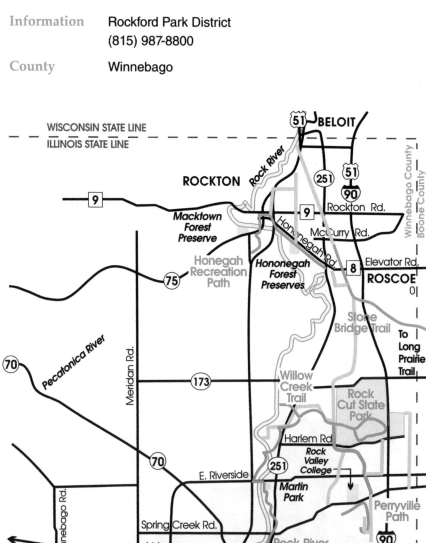

Algonquin Road Trail

Trail Length	9.5 miles
Surface	Paved
Location & Setting	The Algonquin Trail is located in northwest Cook County. It runs from Harper College west to Potawami Woods at Stover and Palatine Roads. The trail generally parallels Algonquin Road, but there is a 6 mile loop around the parameter of the Paul Douglas Forest Preserve and the Highland Woods Golf Course south of Algonquin Road. The setting is open and urban, and wooded as you enter the Forest Preserve.
Information	Cook County Forest Preserve (708) 366-9420
County	Cook

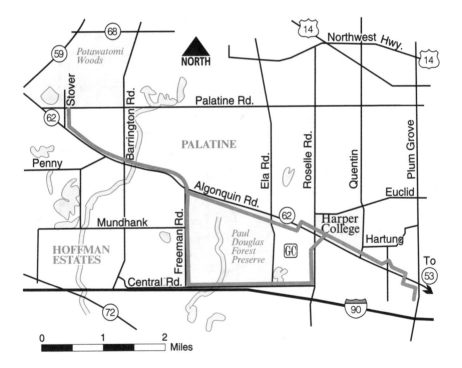

Argyle Lake State Park

Trail Length	7 miles
Surface	Natural – groomed
Location & Setting	From Macomb, west on Rte 136 to Colchester, then north on 500E to the park entrance. Argyle Lake State Park is located about 7 miles west of Macomb, and offers picnicking, camping, and boating in addition to a scenic and rugged 7 mile trail for mountain biking and horseback riding. Effort level is moderate to difficult. There is a concession stand near the boat dock. Class, A, B, C and D campsites are available.
Information	Argyle Lake State Park (309) 776-3422
County	McDonough

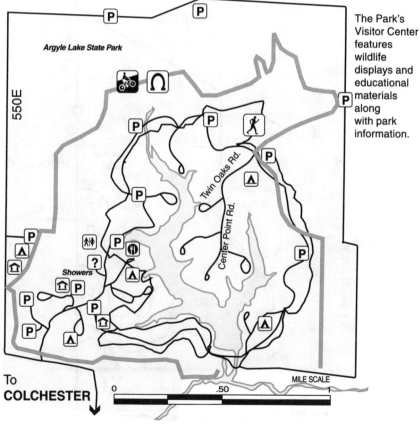

The Park's Visitor Center features wildlife displays and educational materials along with park information.

Arie Crown Bicycle Trail

Trail Length	3.2 miles
Surface	Crushed Gravel
Location & Setting	Located in south Cook County near Countryside and north of the Palos Forest Preserve. Access at Brainard and Joliet Roads or LaGrange Road, north of 67th Street. Woods, open areas.
Information	Forest Preserve District of Cook County (800) 870-3666
County	Cook

EMERGENCY ASSISTANCE
Forest Preserve Police......... (708) 771-1001
or 911

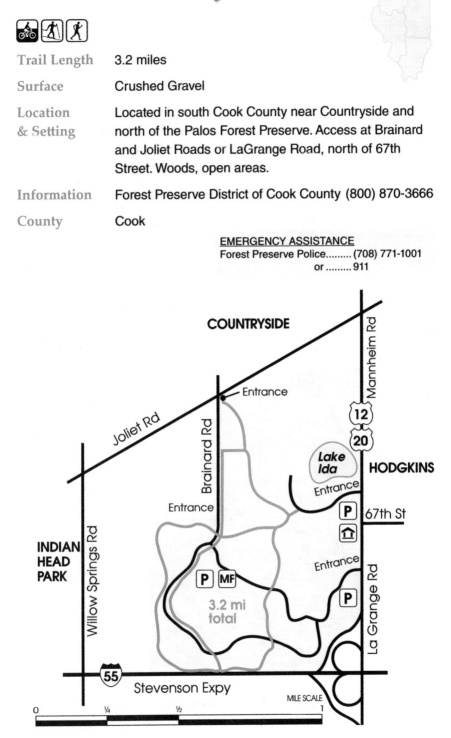

Blackwell Forest Preserve

Trail Length   7.0 miles

Surface   Limestone screenings and mowed turf

Location & Setting   The Blackwell Preserve, located between Winfield and Warrenville in west central DuPage County, can be accessed from Butterfield Road, 1 mile west of Route 59 or from Mack Road, ¼ miles east of Route 59.

Information   Forest Preserve District of DuPage County
(630) 933-7200

County   DuPage

WINFIELD

The Blackwell Preserve has more than 8 miles of multi-purpose trails plus additional footpaths and unmarked trails. The trails lead visitors through a variety of natural settings, including woodlands, marsh and savannas.

MILE SCALE
0   1   2

Wilson St

Gary's Mill Rd

Purnell Rd

Joliet St

59

McKee Marsh

Mack Rd

Williams Rd

Forest View Dr

Springbrook

Mount Hoy

P

P

Silver Lake

Butterfield Rd

?

West Branch DuPage River

WARRENVILLE

56

Illinois Prairie Path

Winfield Rd

FACILITIES

? Info	👭 Restrooms
P Parking	🏠 Shelter

MF Multi Facilities Available

Refreshments	First Aid	Telephone
Picnic	Restrooms	Lodging

Bicyclists are encouraged to stay on the designated trails in the McKee Marsh area on the north end of the Preserve.

Buffalo Creek Forest Preserve

Trail Length	4 miles
Surface	Crushed granite
Location & Setting	Buffalo Creek is a 396 acre preserve near Buffalo Grove and Long Grove on the southern border of Lake County. The trail runs through open area, crossing several creeks, traversing restored prairies, and skirting the reservoir.
	The trail is about 35 miles northwest of the Chicago loop. From I-294, go west Lake Cook Road for 6 miles to Arlington Heights Road, then north a half mile to Checker Road. Go west on Checker Road to the entrance on the south side of the road.
Information	Lake County Forest Preserves (847) 367-6640
County	Lake

Busse Woods Bicycle Trail

Trail Length   11.2 miles

Surface   Paved

Location & Setting   Located in northwest Cook County in the Ned Brown Preserve, bordered on the north by Arlington Heights and to the east by Elk Grove Village. Wooded areas, open spaces and small lakes.

Information   Forest Preserve District of Cook County
(800) 870-3666

County   Cook

The Ned Brown Preserve is a 3,700 acre holding, and surrounds Busse Lake, a 590 acre lake that serves as the focal point of the area.

The bicycle trail winds through the forests and meadows around Busse Lake providing access to many of the preserves unique features.

Trail accesses include Golf Road at Hwy. 90, Arlington Heights Road and Higgins, and at Beisterfield Road and Bisner Road.

ARLINGTON HEIGHTS
MF

Walnut Ave
Central Road
White Oak St
Fernandez Ave
Algonquin Road
Northwest Tollway
Wilke Rd
62
58   Golf Road
290
53
290
72
Higgins Rd
SCHAUMBURG
MF
90
P MF
P MF
P MF
P MF
P MF
P MF
P MF
P MF
ELK GROVE VILLAGE
MF
7.8 mi loop begin/end
Arlington Heights Rd
P
P
P   Bridge
Oakton St
Landmeier Rd
Cosman Rd
Elk Grove Blvd
Bisner Rd
Biesterfield Road

MILE SCALE
0   1

41

Carlyle Lake Prairie View Bike Trail

Trail Length	9.0 miles
Surface	Black top and concrete, with some crushed stone on the eastern end.
Location & Setting	The east trailhead runs from the Carlyle Lake Visitor's Center across the 1.2 mile Carlyle Lake Kaskashas River Dam and the saddle dams, through the countryside to the Boulder Road Trail access. Past the Lake Dam is a rather steep hill cresting just south of the McNair Campground. Restroom facilities are available at the Visitor's Center and the Campground.
Information	US Corps of Engineers (618) 594-2461
County	Clinton

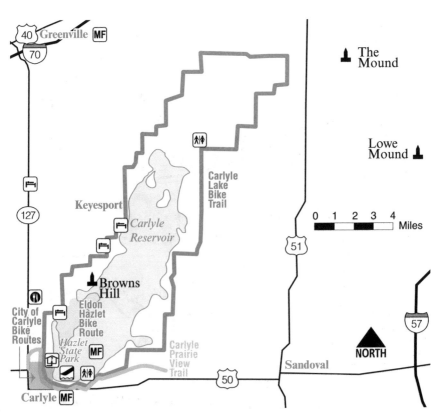

Centennial Trail

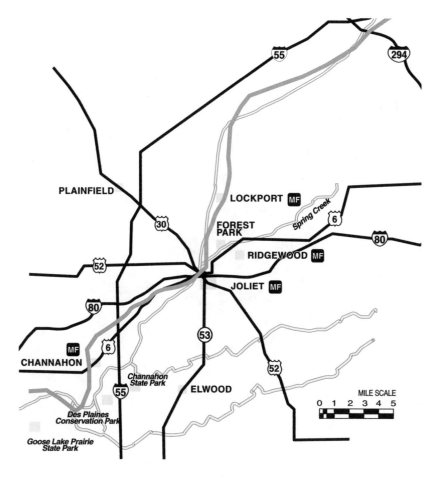

Trail Length	20 miles - planned & partially open
Surface	Paved
Location & Setting	The trail is complete from the Will County line to Willow Springs Road, but still in the planning stages from Willow Spring Road to Harlem. It connects to the Cook County and Will County I&M Canal Trails, and serves as a link to the Grand Illinois Trail. The setting is suburban with most services readily accessible.
Information	Forest Preserve District of Cook County (800) 870-3666
Counties	Cook, DuPage, Will

PLAINFIELD

LOCKPORT MF

55

294

30

FOREST PARK

Spring Creek

6

80

52

RIDGEWOOD MF

JOLIET MF

80

53

52

MF

6

CHANNAHON

Channahon State Park

ELWOOD

Des Plaines Conservation Park

55

Goose Lake Prairie State Park

MILE SCALE
0 1 2 3 4 5

Catlin Park

Trail Length   13 miles

Surface   Natural – groomed

Location & Setting   Catlin Park is located at 2560 E. 1251 Road southwest of Ottawa, and is open from May 1 to October 31 from 9:00am to 7:00pm. There is a $2 daily use or $10 yearly use fee for biking or horseback riding. There are multiple creek crossings, falt areas and several big hills. The trail are multi-use and are well maintained.

Information   LaSalle County Parks Dept.
(815) 434-0518

County   LaSalle

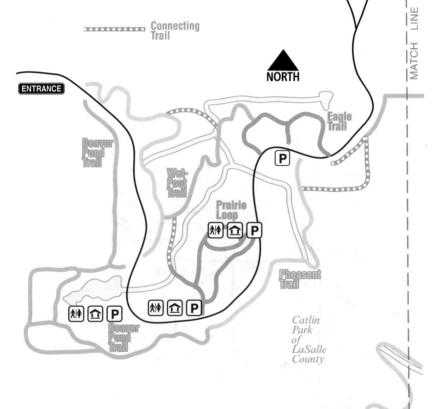

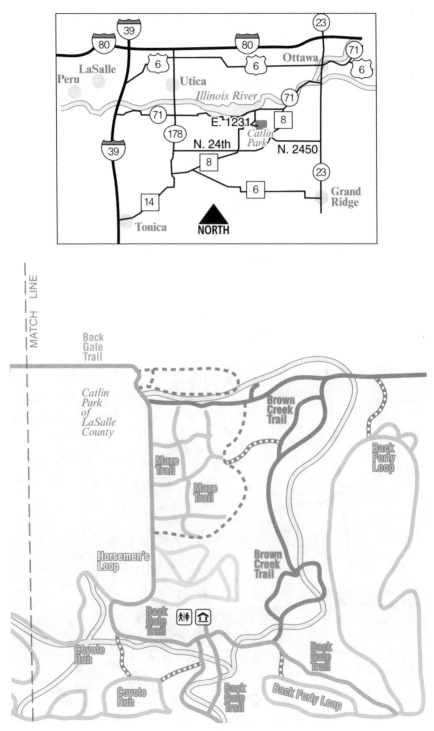

 MATCH LINE

Chain O'Lakes State Park

Trail Length	5.0 miles
Surface	Limestone screenings
Location & Setting	Chain O'Lakes State Park is a 2,793 acre park located at the northwest corner of Lake County. Woods, open park areas.
Information	Chain O'Lakes State Park (847) 587-5512
County	Lake

Summer hours are April 1 through October, from 6 am to 9 pm.

In addition to bicycling, other activities include boating, fishing, picnicking, and camping. Horses and boats can be rented.

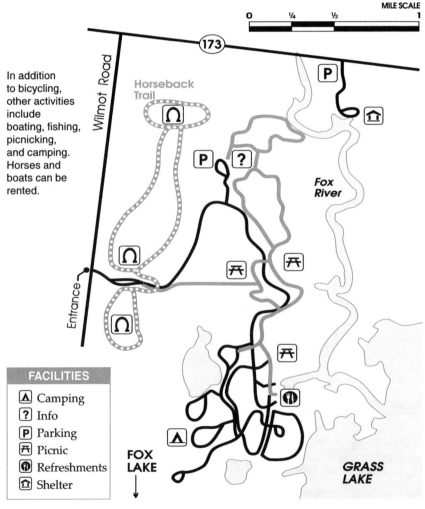

MILE SCALE
0   ¼   ½   1

173

Wilmot Road

Horseback Trail

Fox River

P

?

FACILITIES
- ⓐ Camping
- ? Info
- P Parking
- 🏓 Picnic
- Ⓜ Refreshments
- 🏠 Shelter

Entrance

FOX LAKE

GRASS LAKE

Churchill Woods Forest Preserve

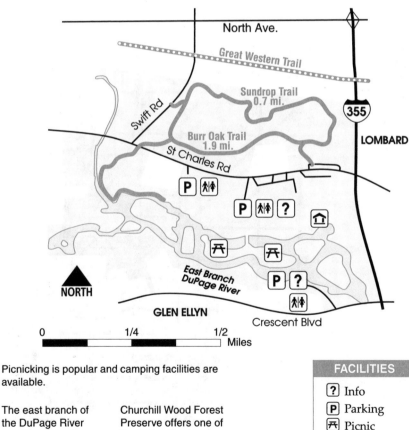

Trail Length	2.5 miles
Surface	Screenings, mowed turf
Location & Setting	The 259 acre preserve is located between Lombard and Glen Ellyn in north central DuPage County. Setting is woodlands, prairie and river.
Information	Forest Preserve District of DuPage County (630) 933-7200
County	DuPage

North Ave.

Great Western Trail

Sundrop Trail 0.7 mi.

Swift Rd

Burr Oak Trail 1.9 mi.

St Charles Rd

355

LOMBARD

P 🚻

P 🚻 ?

🏠

🌲

🌲

East Branch DuPage River

P ?

🚻

NORTH

GLEN ELLYN

Crescent Blvd

0   1/4   1/2
Miles

Picnicking is popular and camping facilities are available.

The east branch of the DuPage River provides more than two miles of waterway frontage.

Churchill Wood Forest Preserve offers one of the last native prairies in DuPage County.

FACILITIES

?	Info
P	Parking
🌲	Picnic
🚻	Restrooms
🏠	Shelter

Chicago Lakefront Bike Path

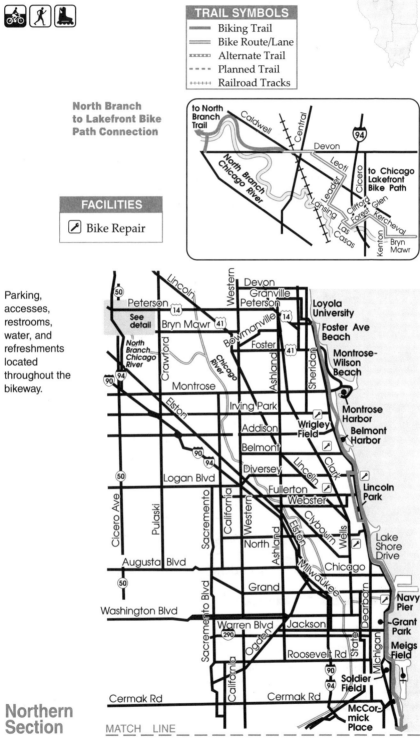

TRAIL SYMBOLS

- ——— Biking Trail
- ═══ Bike Route/Lane
- ▭▭▭ Alternate Trail
- - - - Planned Trail
- +++++ Railroad Tracks

North Branch to Lakefront Bike Path Connection

to North Branch Trail

Caldwell
Central
Devon
94
Leoti
North Branch Chicago River
Leader
Lansing
Las Casas
Cicero
Clifford
Forest
Glen
Kercheval
to Chicago Lakefront Bike Path
Kenton
Bryn Mawr

FACILITIES

🔧 Bike Repair

Parking, accesses, restrooms, water, and refreshments located throughout the bikeway.

Lincoln
50
Peterson
14
See detail
Bryn Mawr
41
North Branch Chicago River
Crawford
90 94
Montrose
Elston
Western
Devon
Granville
Peterson
Bowmanville
Foster
Chicago River
Ashland
14
41
Sheridan
Loyola University
Foster Ave Beach
Montrose-Wilson Beach
Irving Park
Addison
90 94
50
Logan Blvd
Belmont
Diversey
Fullerton
Wrigley Field 🔧
Lincoln 🔧
Clark
Montrose Harbor
Belmont Harbor 🔧
🔧 Lincoln Park
Cicero Ave
Pulaski
Sacramento
California
Western
Ashland
Webster
Clybourn
Elston
Wells
North
Augusta Blvd
50
Sacramento Blvd
Grand
Washington Blvd
Milwaukee
Chicago
Lake Shore Drive
🔧 Navy Pier
Warren Blvd
290
Ogden
Jackson
Dearborn
Grant Park
California
Roosevelt Rd
State
Michigan
Meigs Field
90 94
Soldier Field
Cermak Rd
Cermak Rd
McCormick Place

Northern Section

MATCH LINE

Trail Length	Approximately 20 miles
Surface	Paved
Location & Setting	From the north, the bike path begins around Bryn Mawr (5600 north) and Sheridan Road, then proceeds south along the shoreline of Lake Michigan to 71st Street. Urban lakefront.
Information	Chicago Part District Communications (312) 742-4786
County	Cook

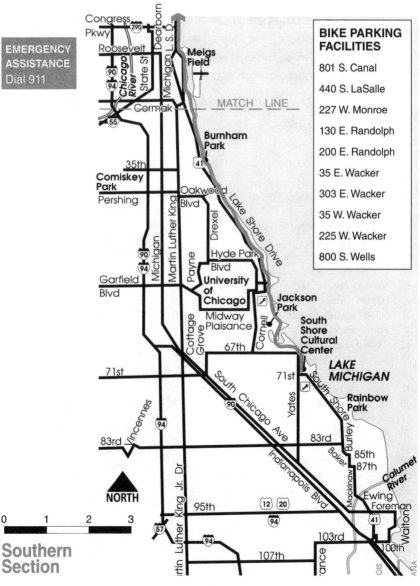

EMERGENCY
ASSISTANCE
Dial 911

BIKE PARKING FACILITIES

801 S. Canal

440 S. LaSalle

227 W. Monroe

130 E. Randolph

200 E. Randolph

35 E. Wacker

303 E. Wacker

35 W. Wacker

225 W. Wacker

800 S. Wells

Southern Section

Constitution Trail

Trail Length	20 miles
Surface	Asphalt
Location & Setting	Located in Bloomington and Normal. The trail is mostly built on abandoned railroad bed through parkways in business and residential areas. The north/south segment is wooded with patches of prairie. Trail access from numerous street connections. Picnic tables and benches are located along the trails. Both Illinois State University and Wesleyan University are located within a short distance of the trail.
Information	Bloomington Parks & Recreation Dept (309) 454-9540
County	McClean

ID	Trailhead	Facilities
1.	Atwood Wayside / Herb Garden	🍴 🏠 P 🚻 🍴 POI HS
2.	Davis Mansion/Jefferson St. Historic Dist.	P POI HS
3.	Historic Franklin Park	🍴 P B POI HS
4.	Children's Discovery Museum	P POI
5.	Camelback Bridge	🍴 🍴 HS B POI
6.	Rest Area (Allers Shelter)	🍴 🏠 🍴 B POI
7.	Normal Parks & Recreation Office	P
8.	Normal City Hall Access	🍴 P B
9.	Hidden Creek Natural Wayside	🍴 P 🍴 B POI
10.	Rose Parks Commons	🍴 🏠 P 🚻 🍴 B
11.	Kerrick Road	🍴 P B
12.	Colene Hoose School Access\Natural Prairie	🍴 P POI
13.	Audubon Garden	🚻 B POI
14.	Sister Cities Gardens	🍴 🚻 🚲 B
15.	Natural Prairie Site	POI
16.	G.E. Road Access	P
17.	Tipton Park	🍴 🏠 🍴 🚻 B
18.	Rollingbrook Park	🍴 🏠 🍴 P 🚻
19.	Brookridge Park	🍴 🏠 🍴 P 🚻
20.	Clearwater Park	🍴 🏠 🍴 P 🚻
21.	Bloomington Parks & Recreation Office	P
22.	Pepper Ridge Park	🍴 🏠 🍴 P 🚻 B
23.	West Route 9 Wayside	P 🚻
24.	Alton Depot Park	🍴 B
25.	Carden Park	🍴 🏠 P 🚻 🍴 B
26.	Fairview Park	🍴 🏠 P 🚻 🍴 🚲
27.	McGraw Park	🍴 🏠 P 🚻 🍴 🚲

FACILITIES

P	Parking
🛆	Picnic
🍴	Refreshments
🚻	Restrooms
🏠	Shelter
🚰	Water
HS	Historical Site
POI	Point of Interest
B	Beach

The trail is built on abandoned trail bed and runs through business and residential areas. The north/south segment is wooded with patches of prairie on the eastern section. Trail accesses from numerous street connections.

Picnic tables and benches are located along the trail. Both Illinois State University and Wesleyan University are located within a short distance of the trail.

Open from dawn to dusk.

Comlara Park

Trail Length	12.0 miles
Surface	Natural turf
Location & Setting	Located approximately 12 miles north of Normal. Take Hwy 39 north to Rte 8 (2500N), then west to the park. There are nearly 8 miles of singletrack and 4 miles of more open and wider county trails encompassing the northwestern part of Evergreen Lake. Setting is wooded with lakefront and hills. No water or restrooms are available on these trails.
Information	McLean County Parks and Recreation (309) 726-2022
County	McLean

Trail	Miles	Effort Level
1	0.3	Moderate
2	0.7	Moderate
3	1.0	Moderate
4	0.4	Easy
5	0.5	Difficult
6	0.7	Moderate
Coharie Pass	0.3	Moderate
7	0.7	Moderate
Bovine Run	1.0	Moderate
Hillside	1.0	Difficult
County Trails	4.0	Easy

Downhill Prelude

Bovine Run

E. 2500 N. Rd.

———— Singletrack Biking Trail

••••••••• County Biking Trail

Evergreen Lake

Coharie Pass

Ropp Rd.

NORTH

Cuba Marsh Forest Preserve

Trail Length	3.0 miles
Surface	Crushed gravel
Location & Setting	This 792-acre marsh offers a diversity of marsh and prairie with woodland and savanna. The ride takes you through open areas of gently rolling hills that feature views of the marsh and scattered groves of trees. The marsh supports several endangered species of plants and birds.
Information	Lake County Forest Preserves (847) 367-6640
County	Lake

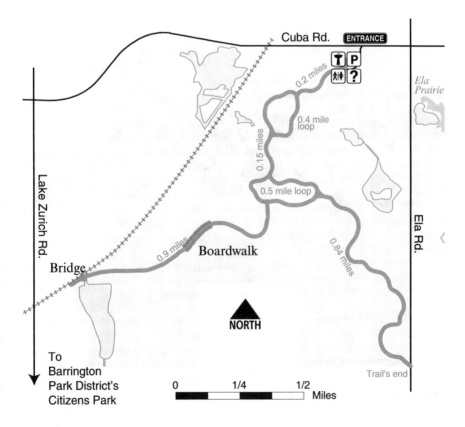

Danada Forest Preserve

Trail Length	2.8 miles of bicycle trails, 3.6 miles total
Surface	Limestone screenings
Location & Setting	Danada Forest Preserve located in the city of Wheaton in central DuPage County, can be accessed from Naperville Road, ½ mile north of Interstate 88. Prairie, woodland, and marsh.
Information	Forest Preserve Dist. of DuPage County (630) 933-7200
County	DuPage

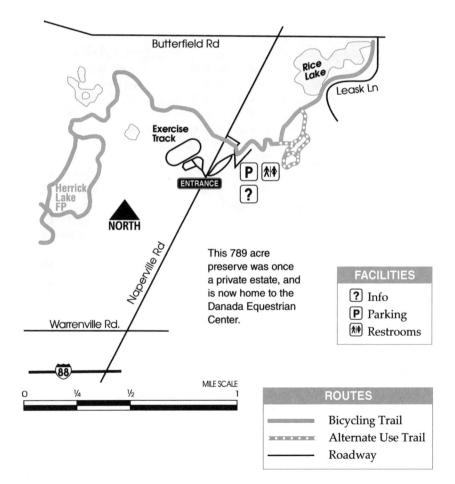

Butterfield Rd

Rice Lake

Leask Ln

Exercise Track

P 👫

ENTRANCE

?

Herrick Lake FP

▲ NORTH

Naperville Rd

This 789 acre preserve was once a private estate, and is now home to the Danada Equestrian Center.

Warrenville Rd.

88

MILE SCALE
0   ¼   ½   1

FACILITIES
? Info
P Parking
👫 Restrooms

ROUTES
Bicycling Trail
Alternate Use Trail
Roadway

Decatur Area Trails

Trail Length	6 miles
Surface	Paved & gravel
Location & Setting	The setting is parkland, lakes, open spaces, and woods. The park is open from 7 am to sunset. The trail winds through Fairview Park, crosses Stevens Creek, through to Kiwanis Park and Sunset Avenue ending at the Rock Springs Environmental Center. It follows the Sangamon River, Lake Decatur, and Stevens Creek.
	Decatur is located in central Illinois west of Springfield on Hwy 32. Parking is available at the Rock Springs Preserve and at Fairview Park. Fairview Park is located at Rte 48 and Hwy 56.
Information	Macon County Conservation District (217) 423-7708
County	Macon

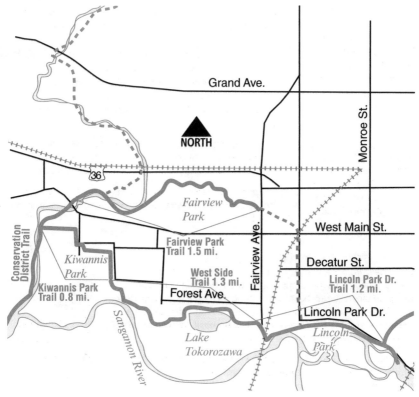

Des Plaines River Trail & Greenway

Trail Length	31.0 miles
Surface	Limestone screenings
Location & Setting	The Des Plaines River Trail parallels its namesake river through Lake County. Open area such as prairies and savannas are common. As you travel through this river valley, look for changes in the landscape. In northern Lake County, the valley is wide and the river meanders. In southern Lake County, the valley is narrow and the river runs a straighter course. Woodlands are more common.
Information	Lake County Forest Preserves (847) 367-6640
County	Lake

From Lake Cook Road northbound you'll pass through Half Day and Wright Woods Forest Preserves, then MacArthur Woods, Old School Forest Preserves, Independence Grove and finally around Sterling Lake before ending at Russell Road at the Wisconsin State Line.

Right-of-Way Laws

When you come to a stop sign at a two-way stop intersection, remember that the traffic on the cross street has the right-of-way. You must yield the right-of-way to pedestrians and vehicles on the cross street before you go ahead.

Blind, hearing impaired or physically handicapped persons can be identified by their white canes, support or guide dogs. You must always yield the right-of-way to them.

If a policeman directs otherwise, the right-of-way laws do not apply and riders and pedestrians must do as the officer tells them.

TRAIL SYMBOLS

- ▬▬ Biking Trail
- ══ Bike Route/Lane
- ▭▭▭ Alternate Trail
- ╴╴╴ Planned Trail
- ┼┼┼┼ Railroad Tracks

Lake County Forest Preserves

Open daily from 8 am to sunset daily. Alcoholic beverages may not be consumed in or near parking areas. Pets are permitted, except in picnic areas, but must be controlled on a leash (no longer than 10 feet). Forest Preserve Ranger Police regularly patrol the Preserves. Ranger Police receive the same basic training as other Illinois police officers and have the same authority.

More than 25,000 acres make up the Lake County Forest Preserves, a dynamic and unique system of natural and cultural resources.

FACILITIES

- **?** Info
- **P** Parking
- **⛬** Picnic
- **🍴** Refreshments
- **🚻** Restrooms
- **⌂** Shelter
- **💧** Water

Northern Section

Access the northern section just south of the state line, on Russell road east of Route 41; or off US 41, north of IL 173.

Southern Section

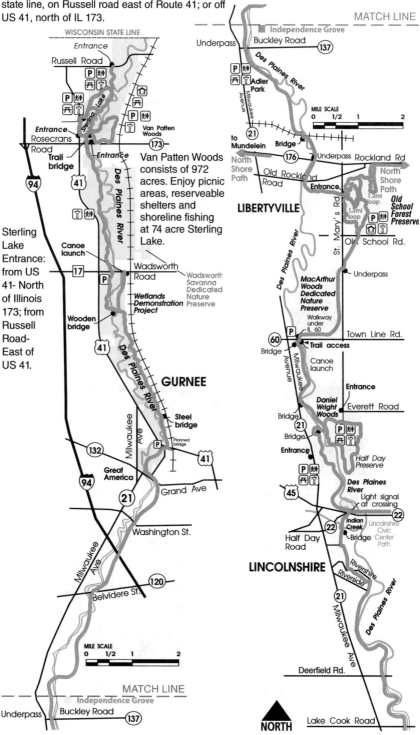

WISCONSIN STATE LINE

Entrance

Russell Road

Entrance
Rosecrans
Road

Trail
bridge

Entrance

Sterling Lake

Van Patten Woods

173

94

41

Van Patten Woods consists of 972 acres. Enjoy picnic areas, reserveable shelters and shoreline fishing at 74 acre Sterling Lake.

Sterling Lake Entrance: from US 41- North of Illinois 173; from Russell Road- East of US 41.

Canoe launch

17

Wadsworth Road

Wetlands Demonstration Project

Wooden bridge

Wadsworth Savanna Dedicated Nature Preserve

Des Plaines River

41

GURNEE

Steel bridge

Planned bridge

132

94

Great America

21

41

Grand Ave

Washington St.

Milwaukee Ave

120

Belvidere St.

Milwaukee Ave

MILE SCALE
0   1/2   1   2

MATCH LINE
Independence Grove

Underpass   Buckley Road   137

MATCH LINE
Independence Grove

Underpass   Buckley Road   137

Des Plaines River

Adler Park

Milwaukee Avenue

to Mundelein
21

Bridge
176   Underpass   Rockland Rd

North Shore Path   Old Rockland Road   Entrance

North Shore Path

1.2mi loop
1.3mi loop

Old School Forest Preserve

P

LIBERTYVILLE

St. Mary's Rd

Old School Rd.

Underpass

Des Plaines River

MacArthur Woods Dedicated Nature Preserve

Walkway under IL 60

60
Bridge

P   Trail access   Town Line Rd.

Milwaukee Avenue

Canoe launch

Entrance

Daniel Wright Woods   Everett Road

P

Bridge
21

Bridge   Entrance   Half Day Preserve

Des Plaines River

P

45

Light signal at crossing

Indian Creek   Lincolnshire Civic Center Path
22   Bridge

22   Half Day Road

LINCOLNSHIRE

Rivershire
Riverside

21

Des Plaines River

Milwaukee Ave

Deerfield Rd.

MILE SCALE
0   1/2   1   2

NORTH   Lake Cook Road

Des Plaines TrailSystem North

Trail Length	12 miles
Surface	Natural groomed (5 to 10 feet wide)
Location & Setting	Located along the east bank of the Des Plaines River in northwest Cook County. It begins at Touhy Avenue, east of Mannheim Road, and continues north to the Lake-Cook County line. The setting is river bottom with woods, open areas and small hills.
Information	Cook County Forest Preserve District (800) 870-3666
County	Cook

Northern Section

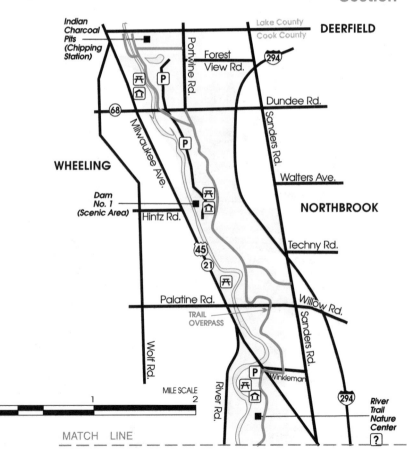

TRAIL SYMBOLS
Biking Trail
Bike Route/Lane
Alternate Trail
Planned Trail
Railroad Tracks

FACILITIES
+ First Aid
? Info
P Parking
Picnic
Shelter

Southern Section

There is a trail gap between Northwest Hwy. and Rand Road. Take the Des Plaines River Road for half a mile and then east on Algonquin Rd. to pick up the trail again.

The Des Plaines River Division has some 4,100 acres enveloping the Des Plaines River Valley.

Des Plaines TrailSystem South

Trail Length	10 .8 miles
Surface	Natural groomed
Uses	Fat tire bicycling, hiking, horseback riding
Location & Setting	Located along the east bank of the Des Plaines River in northwest Cook County. The trail begins at Madison Street, east of First Avenue in Maywood, and follows the Des Plaines River north to Touhy Avenue, east of the Tri-State Tollway in Des Plaines.
Information	Cook County Forest Preserve District (800) 870-3666
County	Cook

FACILITIES

- ✚ First Aid
- ？ Info
- Ｐ Parking
- 🎪 Picnic
- 🏠 Shelter

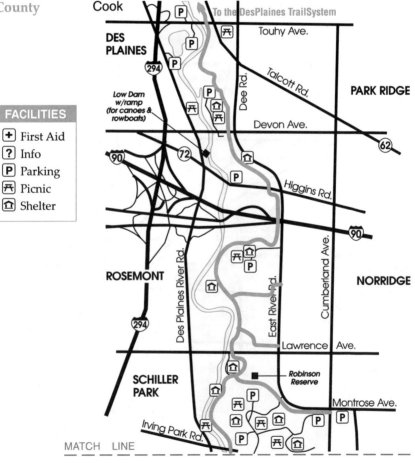

To the DesPlaines TrailSystem

DES PLAINES

Touhy Ave.

294

Low Dam w/ramp (for canoes & rowboats)

Dee Rd.

Talcott Rd.

PARK RIDGE

Devon Ave.

62

90

72

Higgins Rd.

90

ROSEMONT

Des Plaines River Rd.

Cumberland Ave.

NORRIDGE

294

East River Rd.

Lawrence Ave.

Robinson Reserve

SCHILLER PARK

Montrose Ave.

Irving Park Rd.

MATCH LINE

The trail connects to the Salt Creek Forest Preserve to the south and to the Des Plaines River Division to the north.

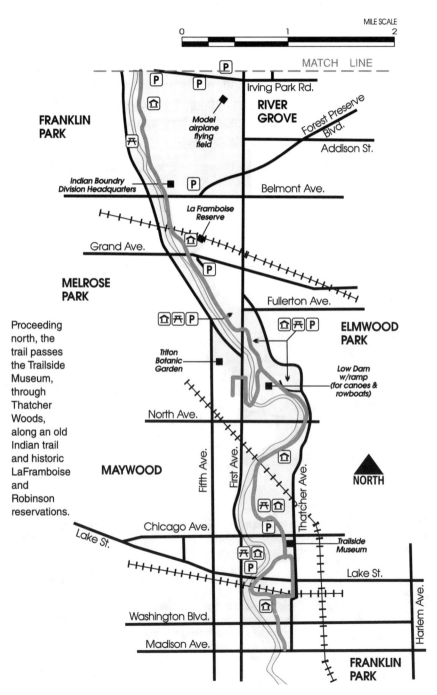

MILE SCALE

0   1   2

MATCH   LINE

Irving Park Rd.

FRANKLIN PARK

RIVER GROVE

Forest Preserve Blvd.

Addison St.

Model airplane flying field

Indian Boundry Division Headquarters

Belmont Ave.

La Framboise Reserve

Grand Ave.

MELROSE PARK

Fullerton Ave.

ELMWOOD PARK

Triton Botanic Garden

Low Dam w/ramp (for canoes & rowboats)

Proceeding north, the trail passes the Trailside Museum, through Thatcher Woods, along an old Indian trail and historic LaFramboise and Robinson reservations.

North Ave.

Fifth Ave.

First Ave.

Thatcher Ave.

NORTH

MAYWOOD

Chicago Ave.

Lake St.

Trailside Museum

Lake St.

Harlem Ave.

Washington Blvd.

Madison Ave.

FRANKLIN PARK

Deer Grove Trail System

Trail Length & Surface	Paved	2.8 miles (Red Trail Loop)
	Unpaved	10.8 miles (Black, Yellow, Orange & Brown Trails)

Location & Setting
The Deer Grove Preserve consists of rolling upland forest interspersed with wooded ravines and wetlands. Creeks meander through the tract, feeding two lakes located in the preserve. Open spaces, wooded areas (connects to Palatine Trail).

Information
Forest Preserve District of Cook County (800) 870-3666

County
Cook

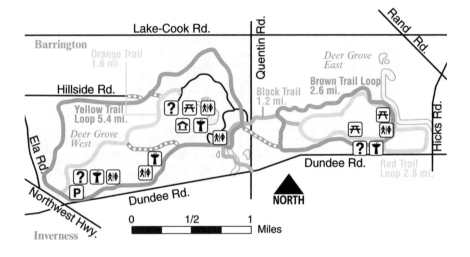

There are several picnic areas located in Deer Grove East. The Deer Grove Bicycle Trail links with the Palatine Trail at Quentin and Dundee Roads. Access to the trail can be gained at both Deer Grove and Deer Grove East parking facilities.

TRAIL SYMBOLS

— Biking Trail
= Bike Route/Lane
▭▭▭ Alternate Trail
- - - - Planned Trail
++++++ Railroad Tracks

You can ride through a mature forest past a herd of elk, then head for the lake to watch the sailboats. There are six fishing walls if you are inclined to do some fishing along with your bicycling.

FACILITIES

+ First Aid
? Info
P Parking
🎪 Picnic
🏠 Shelter

Edward R. Madigan State Park

Trail Length	7 miles
Surface	Natural
Location & Setting	This is a scenic 7 mile hiking/biking trail, which meanders through grasses, trees and creek bottoms. The Park is situated on the southern edge of Lincoln, and surrounds the Lincoln Correctional Center and Logan Correctional Center. Facilities include picnic areas and a canoe access to Salt Creek.

From Lincoln, southwest on Rte 66 to the Park entrance on the left. From Springfield, go north on Hwy 55 to Rte 66, then east to the Park. |
| **Information** | Edward R. Madigan State Park (237) 732-1552 |
| **County** | Logan |

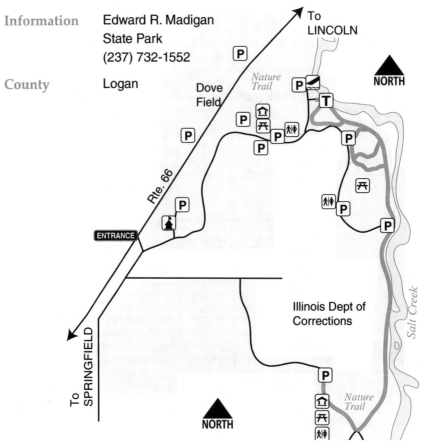

Evanston Bike Paths
North Shore Channel

🚲🛼🚶

Trail Length	7.0 miles
Surface	Paved
Location & Setting	City of Evanston in northeast Cook County north of Chicago and bordering Lake Michigan. Setting is urban, North Shore Channel is open park area.
Information	Evanston Chamber of Commerce (847) 328-1500
County	Cook

EVANSTON- LAKE SHORE PATH TO GREEN BAY TRAIL

Lincoln St. west to Ashland (1 mi.)

Ashland north to Isabella (.4 mi.)

Isabella west to Poplar Dr. (.4 mi.)

Poplar Dr. north to Forest Ave. (1 mi.)

EMERGENCY ASSISTANCE

Dial 911

▲
NORTH

1.25 mi. to Green Bay Trail

EVANSTON

Isabella St

Central

Lincoln

Grant

Simpson

Hartrey

Green Bay Rd.

Dyche Stadium

Asbury Ave

Sheridan Rd.

Noyes

Ridge Ave

North Shore Channel

Emerson

3.75 mi to No. Branch Trail

Church

Lake

Dempster

McDaniel Ave

Dodge Ave

Main

Asbury Ave

Ridge Ave

Orrington Ave

North-western Univ.

Lake

Lake Front Park

Eliot Park

Main

Kedzie

Keeney

S. Blvd.

Custer

Sheridan

Lake Michigan

Calvary Cemetery

No. Shore Channel

Oakton

3 miles to Chicago Lakefront Bikeway

Fermilab Bike Trail

Trail Length	4.0 miles
Surface	Paved
Location & Setting	The east access is off Batavia Road just west of Hwy. 59. The west access is off Kirk Road about ¾ miles north of Butterfield Road. Tall grass prairie, flood plain woods and wetlands.
Information	Batavia Park District (630) 879-5235
County	DuPage

As an alternate, tour the scenic 4 mile trail through Fermilab, or extend it to a 14 mile round trip by way of the Aurora Branch, Batavia Spur and paved paths along Kirk Road and Batavia Road.

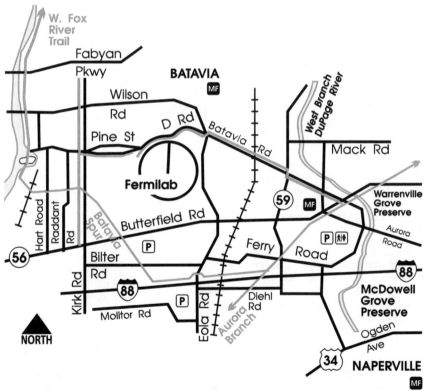

You can learn about everything from subatomic particles to bison at Fermilab. Built in the 1950's, Fermilab is on the cutting edge of particle acceleration research. However, don't miss the woods, ponds, and prairie. The top floor (15th) is open for observation, and can provide a spectacular view of the Fox Valley.

Fox River Trail

Trail Length	41.7 miles
Surface	Paved, limestone screenings
Location & Setting	Follows the Fox River between Crystal Lake and Aurora. Open spaces and small communities.
Information	Fox Valley Park District (630) 897-0516
	Dundee Township Tourist Center (847) 426-2255
County	McHenry, Kane

Northward from Oswego, this trail winds through the Fox River Valley running northward from Aurora to Crystal Lake. You'll bike through forest and nature preserves, and several historic and interesting communities. This popular trail connects to the Illinois Prairie Path to the east, to the Great Western Trail west of St. Charles and to the Virgil Gilman Trail in Aurora. Plans include extending the trail via bikeways through Crystal Lake, then connecting to the Prairie Trail (north section) which will continue to the Wisconsin state line.

Red Oak Nature Center is a 40 acre oak and maple forest on the east bank of the Fox River. Inside the nature center building, you'll find a contemporary museum stressing the four basic elements of life...sun, air, water and soil.

Devil's Cave is one of the most unusual natural features on the trail. Although small, this is one of the very few caves in northeastern Illinois. Rich in folklore, this cave is believed to have been used by the Pottawatomie Indians.

ROUTE SLIP	SEGMENT	TOTAL
Crystal Lake Ave – Crystal Lake		0.0
Botz Rd - Carpentersville	7.0	7.0
Hwy 72/68 – E. Dundee	4.0	11.0
Hwy 90 – Elgin	3.5	14.5
Hwy 20 – Elgin	5.1	19.6
River Crossing – S. Elgin	2.9	22.5
Army Trail Rd – St. Charles	4.7	27.2
State St. – Geneva	5.0	32.2
Hwy 88	7.5	39.5
Illinois Ave. – Aurora	2.0	41.5
River Crossing – Oswego	7.5	49.0

FACILITIES

- ⚒ Bike Repair
- ✚ First Aid
- ⃤ Info
- ⊟ Lodging
- Ⓟ Parking
- ⊞ Picnic
- ⓪ Refreshments
- ⚥ Restrooms
- ⌂ Shelter
- MF Multi Facilities Available

Refreshments	First Aid
Telephone	Picnic
Restrooms	Lodging

For information concerning trail activities, please contact:
Illinois Department of Natural Resources Office of Resource
Marketing and Education
524 S. Second St.
Springfield, IL 62701-1787
(217)782-7454

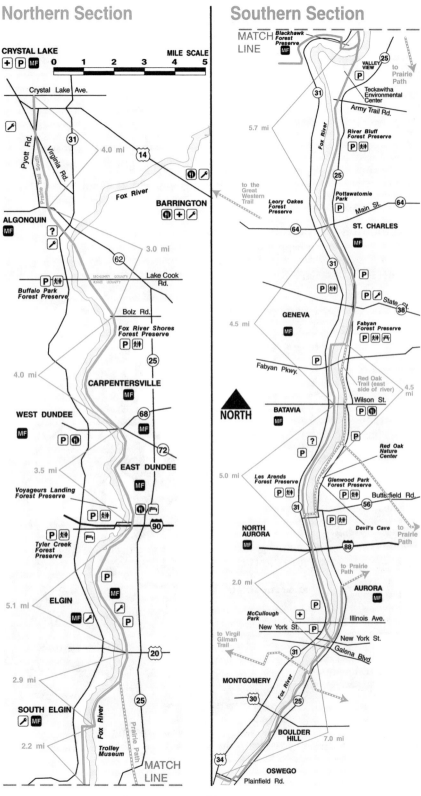

Fullersburg Forest Preserve

Trail Length	3.8 miles
Surface	Crushed limestone
Location & Setting	Located between Oak Brook and Hinsdale in east central DuPage County, Fullersburg Forest Preserve can be accessed from Spring Road, ½ mile northwest of York Road. Woodlands, prairie, creek crossings.
Information	Forest Preserve District of DuPage County (630) 933-7200
County	Du Page

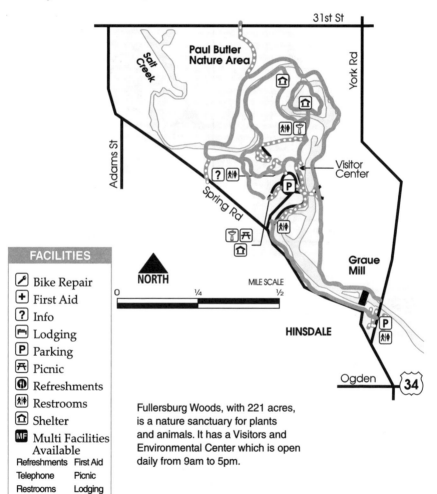

FACILITIES

- 🔧 Bike Repair
- ➕ First Aid
- ❓ Info
- 🛏 Lodging
- 🅿 Parking
- 🍽 Picnic
- 🍴 Refreshments
- 🚻 Restrooms
- 🏠 Shelter
- **MF** Multi Facilities Available

Refreshments   First Aid
Telephone   Picnic
Restrooms   Lodging

Fullersburg Woods, with 221 acres, is a nature sanctuary for plants and animals. It has a Visitors and Environmental Center which is open daily from 9am to 5pm.

Fulton Bike Trail (F.A.S.T.)

Trail Length	6 miles existing, 8+ miles planned
Surface	Asphalt, shared streets
Location & Setting	Located in Fulton along the Mississippi River in northwest Illinois. Setting is riverfront, city streets.
Information	Fulton Chamber of Commerce (815) 589-4545
County	Whiteside

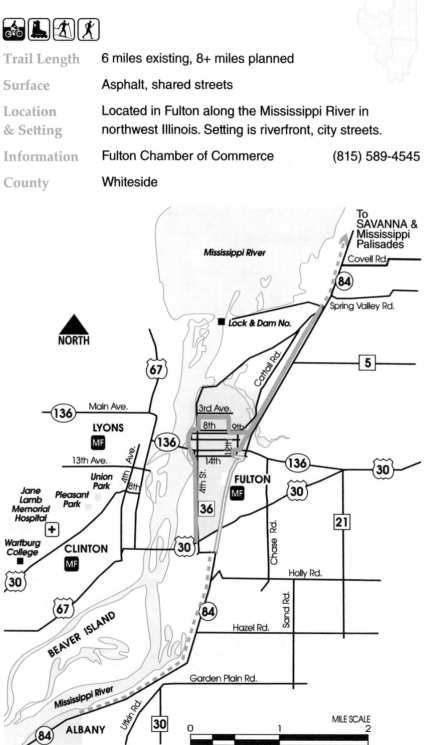

Grand Illinois Trail

Trail Length	**535 miles**
Location & Setting	Existing and planned trails, forming a loop of northern Illinois, from the suburbs of Chicago to the Mississippi and from the Wisconsin border to the I&M and Hennepin Canals. A series of trails and road segments, with some of the proposed route still conceptual with linkages to trails via lightly traveled roads and streets.
Information	Grand Illinois Trail Coordinator (815-732-9072)
County	Covers 18 counties

A series of 17 trails and road segments covering several hundred miles looping Northern Illinois. Some of the proposed route is still conceptual, with linkages to trails via lightly traveled roads and streets.

TRAIL SYMBOLS

- Biking Trail
- Bike Route/Lane
- Alternate Trail
- Planned Trail
- Railroad Tracks

NORTH

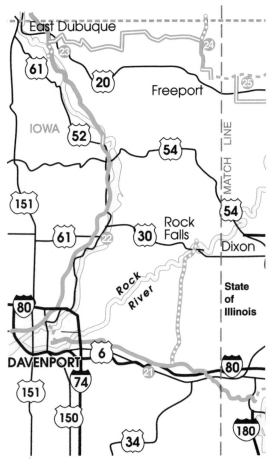

GRAND ILLINOIS TRAIL SYSTEM SEGMENTS

1	McClory Trail	14	Prairie Trail
2	Green Bay Trail	15	Fox River Trail
3	North Branch Trail	16	Great Western Trail
4	Lake Front Path	17	Dekalb-Sycamore Trail
5	Burnham Greenway	18	DuPage River Trail
6	Old Plank Road Trail	19	I&M Canal State Trail
7	North Shore Path	20	Kaskaskia Alliance Trail
8	Des Plaines River Trail	21	Hennepin Canal State Trail
9	Illinois Prairie Path	22	Great River Trail
10	Centennial Trail	23	Galena River Trail
11	I&M Canal Trails	24	Jane Addams Trail
12	Wauponsee Glacial Trail	25	Pecatonica Prairie Path
13	Hebron Trail	26	Rock River Recreation Path
		27	Long Prairie Trail

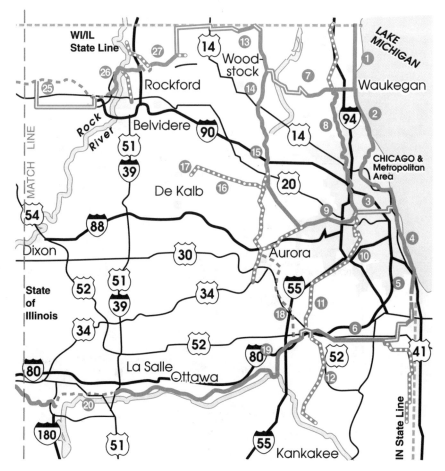

Grant Woods Forest Preserve

Trail Length   6.0 miles

Surface   Limestone screenings

Location   Grant Woods is east of Fox Lake and bounded by Rte.
& Setting   59 on the west, Rte. 83 on the east, Rte. 132 north and
Rte. 134 south. Enter on Monaville Rd. east of Rte. 59.
The northern half is largely marsh and prairie.

Information   Lake County Forest Preserve   (847) 367-6640

County   Lake

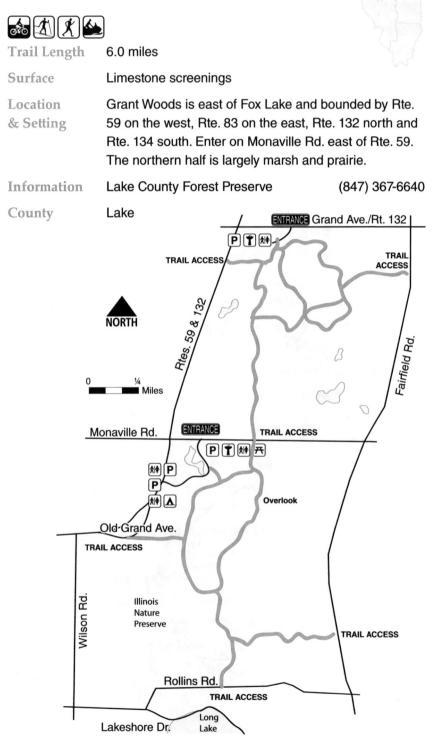

Great Western Trail

Trail Length	18 miles
Surface	Limestone screenings
Location & Setting	This 18 mile trail extends from the LeRoy Oakes Forest Preserve west of St. Charles to Sycamore at Old State and Airport Road in Kane and DeKalb counties and stands on the former site of the Chicago and Northwestern Railroad line. Rural landscape, wetlands, farmlands, small communities.
Information	Kane County Forest Preserve (630) 232-5980
County	DeKalb, Kane

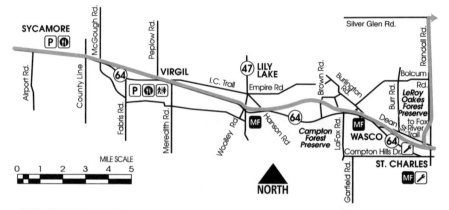

FACILITIES

- 🔧 Bike Repair
- ➕ First Aid
- ❓ Info
- 🏨 Lodging
- 🅿 Parking
- 🎪 Picnic
- 🍴 Refreshments
- 🚻 Restrooms
- 🏠 Shelter
- **MF** Multi Facilities Available

Refreshments	First Aid
Telephone	Picnic
Restrooms	Lodging

There is a bike route from the city of DeKalb to a nature trail. The Peace Road Trail links DeKalb and Sycamore with a recreational path.

The Great Western Trail is a rail-to-trails conversion. Horseback riding is permitted from Lily Lake to LeRoy Oakes. Snowmobiling is permitted with 4 or more inches of snow.

There are plans to provide a 3.5 mile corridor between the Fox River Trail and the Great Western Trail. The path will run south from Silver Glen Road along Randall Road on a county highway easement to LeRoy Oakes Forest Preserve, where it will connect with the Great Western Trail.

Great River Trail
Ben Butterworth Parkway

Trail Length	62.0 miles
Surface	Paved paths (10 feet), shared streets, undeveloped
Location & Setting	The Great River Trail will eventually run from Rock Island to the Mississippi Palisades State Park, north of Savanna, along the Mississippi River in northwest Illinois. The setting is riverfront, urban to small communities, rural, woods, open areas, farmland.
Information	Bi-State Regional Commission (309) 793-6300 Parks & Recreation Dept. (309) 752-1573 Hampton Village Hall (309) 755-7165
County	Rock Island, Whiteside, Carroll

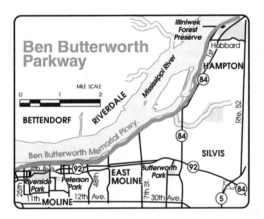

Always lock your bicycle when it is parked. Register your bicycle with your local police department if possible. Be sure to keep your bike's serial number in a safe place.

If you are uncertain of the condition of your bicycle, visit a local bike shop. Most shops offer free safety inspections and books on do-it-yourself maintenance.

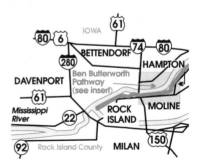

Trailheads

Rock Island   Sunset Park, 18th Avenue and IL Route 92

East Moline   Waterfront & Mississippi Parks (north sides of city)

Hampton   Riverfront Park (south side), Illiniwek Park (north side)

Rapids City   Shuler's Shady Grove Park

Port Byron   Boat access area

Albany   Boat access area

Thomson   Downtown area, Thomson Causeway, Buck's Barn

Savanna   Downtown area
Mississippi Palisades State Park

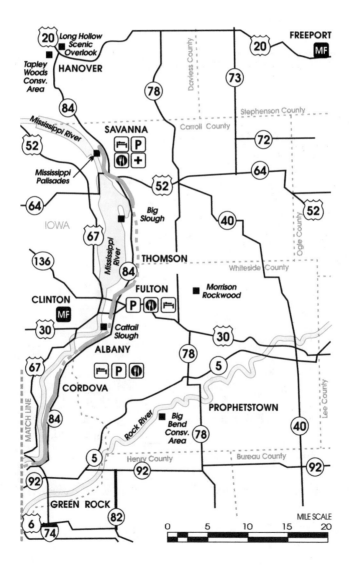

Green Bay Trail

Trail Length	6.0 miles
Surface	Paved
Location & Setting	From Wilmette to the Lake County line, running mostly parallel to the Chicago and Northwestern rail line. Urban setting.
Information	Winnetka Park District (847) 446-0734
County	Cook

This mainly urban to suburban setting provides ample opportunities to enjoy the many eating establishments and beautiful homes along the trail. The south trailhead (Forest Ave. in Wilmette) is 1.2 mi. west of Sheridan Rd. and 2.5 mi. east of I-90/94.

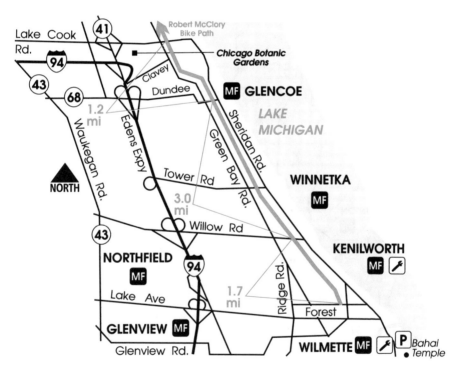

Screenings:

Some of the surface consists of limestone screenings. The remainder is paved, or street/sidewalk connections.

Glencoe   - Scott Ave. & Harbor St. (.4 mi.)

- South Ave. & Hazel Ave. (.2 mi.)

- Maple Hill Rd. & Ravinia Park (1.1 mi.)

Greenbelt Forest Preserve

Trail Length	4.3 miles of looped trails
Surface	Crushed gravel
Location & Setting	The Greenbelt Forest Preserve is nestled between the cities of Waukegan and North Chicago, east of Route 41 and south of Route 120.
Information	Lake County Forest Preserve (847) 367-6640
County	Lake

Entrances- West Section: off Green Bay Road (Route 131) & 12th Street (open May - Nov) East Section: Dugdale Road, south of 10th Street (open year round).

WAUKEGAN

Belvedere Road

120

Greenbay Road

131

10th Street

.75 mi lake loop

NORTH

41

1.3 mi loop

1.5 mi loop

P

ENTRANCE

P

12th Street

.7 mi loop

Greenbelt Cultural Center

Dugdale Road

Lewis Avenue

14th Street

MILE SCALE

0   ½   1

NORTH CHICAGO

Greene Valley Forest Preserve

Trail Length	10.0 miles
Surface	Gravel, mowed turf
Location & Setting	Greene Valley Forest Preserve is located in far south central DuPage County, on Greene Road, ½ mile south of 75th Street. 1,400 acres of woodlands and grasslands.
Information	Forest Preserve District of DuPage County (630) 933-7200
County	DuPage

Trails are symbol coded and may be traveled in both directions. Loop trails range from 1.75 to 6.25 miles.

Access on:
Thunderbird Road
70th Street
Greene Road between Hobson Road and 75th Street.

Herrick Lake Forest Preserve

Trail Length	6.5 miles
Surface	Limestone screenings
Location & Setting	Located in central DuPage County, between Winfield and Naperville. Access from Herrick Road or Butterfield Road. Herrick Lake has 760 acres with a 21 acre lake.
Information	Forest Preserve District of DuPage County (630) 933-7200
County	DuPage

WINFIELD

WHEATON

Weisbrook Rd.

Orchard Rd.

Butterfield Rd.

56

Arrowhead Golf Course
Wheaton Park District

56

WARRENVILLE

Herrick Rd.

P

Park Ranger

To
Danada
Forest
Preserve

Meadowlark
Trail

Galusha Ave.

Bluebird Trail

Warrenville Rd.

Mill St.

Green Heron
Trail

Indian Hill Dr.

Naperville Rd.

88

88

Diehl

NORTH

NAPERVILLE

0   1/2   1   Miles

There is a concession building on the eastern shore of the lake. Canoes and row boats are available for rental.

Hennepin Canal Parkway

Trail Length	98 miles
Surface	Paved
Location & Setting	The Hennepin Canal Parkway is a unique linear waterway corridor in northwestern Illinois. The main line of the waterway extends from the great bend of the Illinois River to the Mississippi River, west of Milan.
Information	Illinois Dept. of Natural Resources (815) 454-2328
Counties	Bureau, Henry, Lee Rock Island, Whiteside.

There are plans to add six miles of trail to connect the Great River Trail along the Mississippi River to the Hennepin Canal Trail.

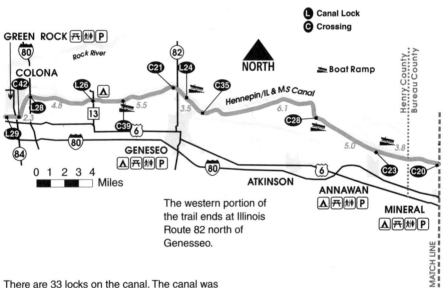

L Canal Lock
C Crossing

GREEN ROCK
COLONA
Rock River
NORTH
Boat Ramp
Hennepin/IL & MS Canal
Henry County/Bureau County
GENESEO
ATKINSON
ANNAWAN
MINERAL
MATCH LINE

0 1 2 3 4 Miles

The western portion of the trail ends at Illinois Route 82 north of Genesseo.

There are 33 locks on the canal. The canal was completed in 1907, but was only used for a short while before being replaced by the railroad.

The parkway is a popular recreatonal area for pleasure boating, picnicking, primitive camping, horseback riding, snowmobiling, backpacking, and hiking in addition to bicycling. A feeder from the Rock River connects to the main line between Sheffield and Mineral. There are numerous parking areas and road accesses along the parkway.

Day-use facilities consists of picnic tables, pit toilets and parking areas. Most of the areas along the canal have these facilities:

Toilets: Locks 11, 17, 21, 22, 23, 24 and bridges 14, 15, 23 and Visitor Center are have toilet facilities.
Water: Drinking water is available at Locks 21, 22 and the Visitor Center area.
Visitor Center: Includes information, displays, flush toilets, drinking water, playground equipment, picnic areas, boat launching ramp & marina.

The parkway extends south 29.3 miles along the feeder canal. Just north of Interstate 80, midway between Routes 78 and 40, the feeder meets the main canal. From this point the parkway runs southwest 46.9 miles to the Mississippi River near Rock Island and southeast 28.4 miles to the Illinois River near the town of Hennepin.

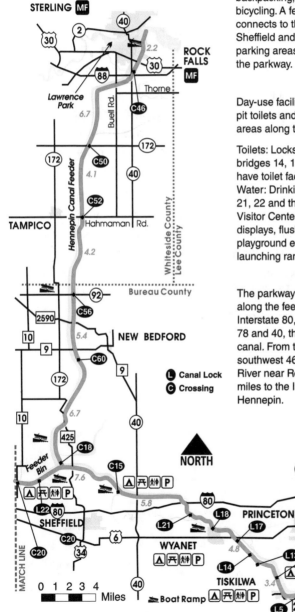

81

Hickory Creek Preserve East & West Branch

🚲🚲🚶⛸️🎿

Trail Length	West Branch	2.8 miles paved, 1 mile natural
	East Branch	1.8 miles

Surface   Asphalt and grass/dirt

Location & Setting   Located south of Modena and north of Frankfort, Hickory Creek is the largest preserve in Will County. The preserve is divided into two sections separated by Wolf Rd.

The West Branch passes through prairie and dense woodlands and crosses Hickory Creek. Parking is available at Hickory Creek Junction, and at the Barrens Creek Barrens on School House Rd. From the Hickory Creek Junction there is access to the Old Plank Rd. Trail.

The East Branch heads south from the La Porte Road parking area, downhill through an open meadow, and then a bridge crossing over Hickory Creek into a forest. Tall oaks line the path. The trail is relatively hilly. Restroom and a water pump are available at the Hickory Hollow Shelter north of the trailhead parking area.

Information   Will County Forest Preserve
(815) 727-8700

County   Will

Brightway Lane

Hickory Creek

Schoolhouse Rd

To NEW LENOX

West Branch

NORTH

To Old Plank Road Trail

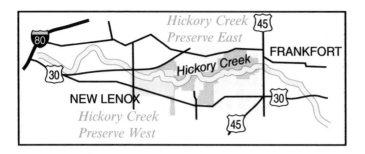

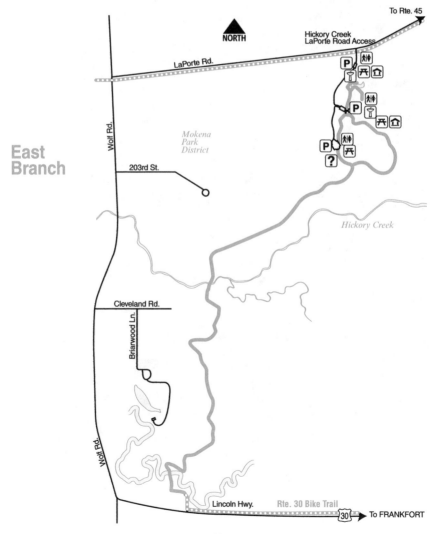

Riding the Des Plaines Division Trail

Hononegah Recreation Path

Trail Length	2.7 miles
Surface	Asphalt
Location & Setting	The path begins at the corner of Elevator Road and Main Street in Roscoe, passes under Hwy. 251, and then parallels the south side of Hononegah Road to Rockton. Open area with small communities at either end.
Information	Rockford Park District (815) 987-8800
County	Winnebago

0   1   2 Miles

ROCKTON

Rockton Rd.

Rock River

Hononegah Rd.

Dorr Rd.

Kelley Myers Park

Second St.

McCurry Rd.

Willowbrook Rd.

Hononegah Forest Preserve

Frances Ln.

Straw Ln.

Cedar-brook Rd.

Rock River

MOREHAVEN   ROSCOE

Second St.

Elevator Rd.

Main Rd.

Pony

Old River Rd.

I & M Canal State Trail

Trail Length	56 miles
Surface	Limestone screenings
Location & Setting	In northeast Illinois, the eastern trailhead begins at the Channanon access. The trail proceeds west to the city of LaSalle, where there are multiple access points and parking. Rural landscape, prairie, small communities
Information	I & M Canal State Trail (815) 942-0796
County	Will, Grundy, LaSalle

BUFFALO ROCK STATE PARK

Directions: Boyce Memorial Drive south to Ottawa Avenue. West 1.8 miles, past Naplate, to the park entrance.Located five miles from the Fox River Aqueduct on the north bank of the Illinois River. Atop the sandstone bluff at the summit of Buffalo Rock is a sweeping view of the Illinois River. It has several picnic areas

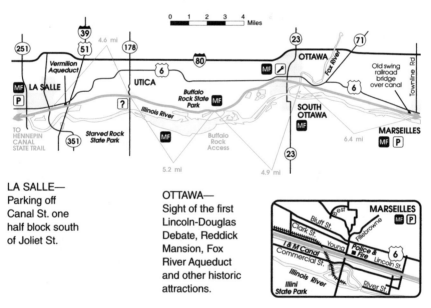

LA SALLE—
Parking off Canal St. one half block south of Joliet St.

OTTAWA—
Sight of the first Lincoln-Douglas Debate, Reddick Mansion, Fox River Aqueduct and other historic attractions.

One of the largest earth sculptures ever built, the Effigy Tumuli is located near the park. This reclaimed mine site has turned a barren wasteland into an area filled with recreational opportunities and interesting landscapes. It contains five large earthen figures (effigies) of native aquatic animals. Represented in geometric forms are a water strider, frog, catfish, turtle and a snake.

The I&M (Illinois and Michigan) Canal provided the first complete water route from the east coast to the Gulf of Mexico by connecting Lake Michigan to the Mississippi River by way of the Illinois River.

Bicyclists can take advantage of the groomed towpath to enjoy the natural and manmade wonders. The trail is marked and has various wayside exhibits that describe features of the canal era.

CHANNANON ACCESS—
Exit Hwy. 6 at Canal St. Proceed one half mile southeast to Story St., then one block west.

AUX SABLE—
This access area is eight miles from Channahon where an aqueduct, lock and locktender's house can be found.

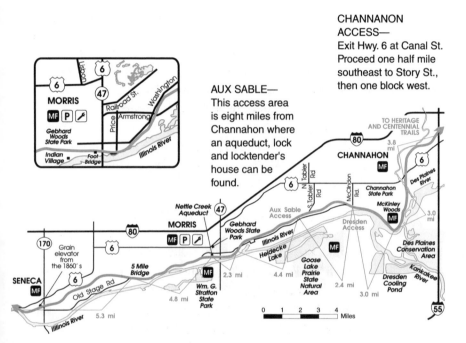

GEBHARD WOODS STATE PARK—
Thirty acres of slightly rolling terrain dotted with many stately shade trees.

WILLIAM G. STRATTON STATE PARK—
Located in Morris, it provides public boat access to the Illinois River. Picnicking and fishing are popular here.

I & M Canal Trail
Will County

Trail Length	11.4 miles
Surface	Asphalt, limestone screenings, packed earth
Location & Setting	This connecting trail consists of three segments. The Centennial Trail extends north of 135th Street for 3 miles along the Des Plaines River to the Cook County border. The Lockport segment extends south from 135th Street through downtown Lockport to Dellwood Park for a total of 5.1 miles. The third segment passes for 3.3 miles along the Joliet Iron Works Historic Site in Joliet. Access to this trail system is at Isle a la Cache and Schneider's Passage in Romeoville, and the Joliet Iron Works Historic Site in Joliet.

Joliet was known as the City of Steel and Stone. Its rich deposits of limestone led to a thriving quarrying industry and a huge iron producing industry for over 60 years until the 1930's. Following the dismantling of the Joliet Iron Works, the foundations of this once bustling factory were finally preserved in the 1990's by the Will County Forest Preserve. There is a 1-mile walkway through the site on a self-guided tour, with exhibits explaining the iron making process. |
| Information | Will County Forest Preserve   (815) 727-8700 |
| County | Will |

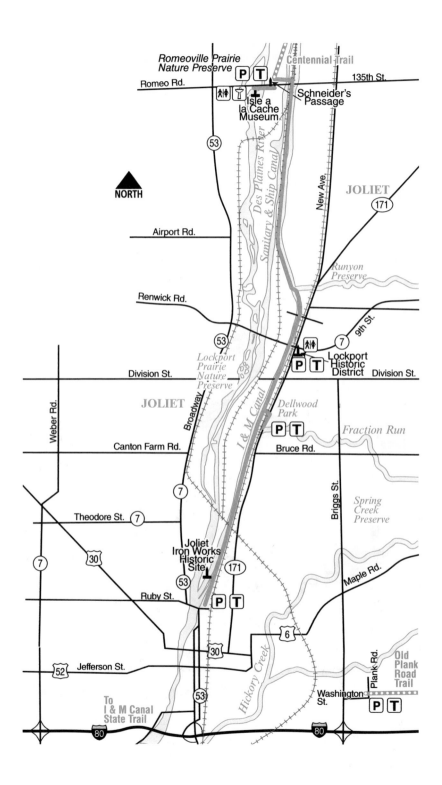

Romeoville Prairie
Nature Preserve

P **T**

Centennial Trail

Romeo Rd.

135th St.

Schneider's
Passage

Isle a
la Cache
Museum

Des Plaines River

Sanitary & Ship Canal

New Ave.

JOLIET

171

▲
NORTH

Airport Rd.

*Runyon
Preserve*

Renwick Rd.

53

9th St.

7

P **T**

Lockport
Historic
District

*Lockport
Prairie
Nature
Preserve*

Division St.

Division St.

JOLIET

Broadway

*Dellwood
Park*

Fraction Run

P **T**

Weber Rd.

Canton Farm Rd.

I & M Canal

Bruce Rd.

Briggs St.

*Spring
Creek
Preserve*

7

Theodore St. 7

Joliet
Iron Works
Historic
Site

30

171

53

Maple Rd.

7

Ruby St.

P **T**

6

30

Hickory Creek

Plank Rd.

Old
Plank
Road
Trail

52 Jefferson St.

53

Washington
St.

P **T**

To
I & M Canal
State Trail

80

80

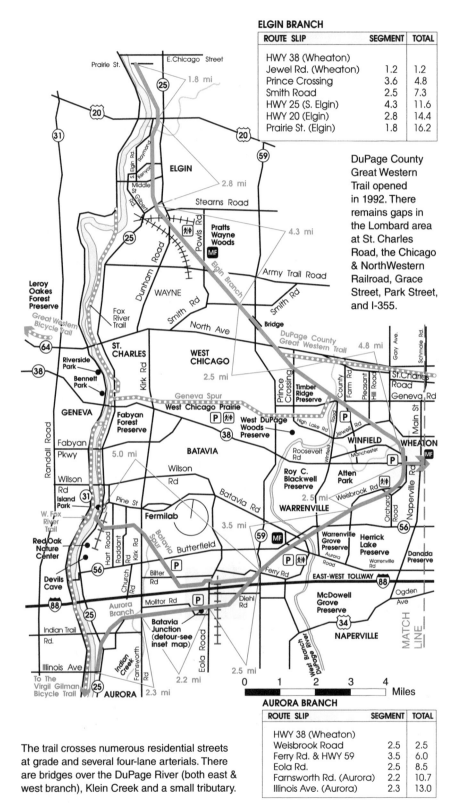

ELGIN BRANCH

ROUTE SLIP	SEGMENT	TOTAL
HWY 38 (Wheaton)		
Jewel Rd. (Wheaton)	1.2	1.2
Prince Crossing	3.6	4.8
Smith Road	2.5	7.3
HWY 25 (S. Elgin)	4.3	11.6
HWY 20 (Elgin)	2.8	14.4
Prairie St. (Elgin)	1.8	16.2

DuPage County Great Western Trail opened in 1992. There remains gaps in the Lombard area at St. Charles Road, the Chicago & NorthWestern Railroad, Grace Street, Park Street, and I-355.

The trail crosses numerous residential streets at grade and several four-lane arterials. There are bridges over the DuPage River (both east & west branch), Klein Creek and a small tributary.

AURORA BRANCH

ROUTE SLIP	SEGMENT	TOTAL
HWY 38 (Wheaton)		
Weisbrook Road	2.5	2.5
Ferry Rd. & HWY 59	3.5	6.0
Eola Rd.	2.5	8.5
Farnsworth Rd. (Aurora)	2.2	10.7
Illinois Ave. (Aurora)	2.3	13.0

Illinois Prairie Path
Batavia and Geneva Spurs
Great Western Trail-DuPage County

Trail Length	Illinois Prairie Path	44.2 miles
	Batavia Spur	5.0 miles
	Geneva Spur	5.0 miles
	Great Western Trail	11.4 miles
Surface	Limestone screenings (Batavia Spur is partially paved)	
Location & Setting	Refer to route slips for location of trails. Prairie, wetlands, open spaces, woods, urban communities.	
Information	County Trail Coordinator	(630) 407-6883
County	Cook, DuPage, Kane	

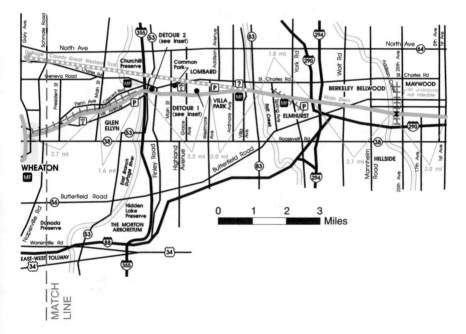

Along much of The Illinois Prairie Path, nature is abundant. Pheasants, flickers, robins, cardinals, chickadees and goldfinch can be found. Many different species of plants are found throughout the seasons. During spring look for mayapples, which look like small green umbrellas popping out of the ground. In summer, violets and onions are in bloom. Autumn brings out goldenrod and asters.

THE ILLINOIS PRAIRIE PATH MAIN STEM

ROUTE SLIP	SEGMENT	TOTAL
HWY 38 (Wheaton)		
Main St. (Glen Ellyn)	2.7	2.7
Du Page River (E. Branch)	1.6	4.3
Westmore Ave. (Lombard)	2.2	6.5
Salt Creek	2.0	8.5
HWY 290 (Elmhurst)	1.8	10.3
Addison Creek	2.7	13.0
First Ave. (Maywood)	2.0	15.0

Illinois Beach State Park

Trail Length	8 miles
Surface	Limestone screenings, packed earth
Location & Setting	Parallels the Lake Michigan shoreline from south of Zion to the Wisconsin State line. Separating the Northern and Southern Units is Commonwealth Edison's power plant. The Northern unit includes the North Point Marina. Additional trail development is planned.

Northern Unit—The path runs from the Marina to San Pond and to the railroad tracks near 7th St. in Winthrop Harbor.

Southern Unit —The path extends along 29th Street to connect to the Zion Bikeway.

Information	Zion Beach State Park (847) 662-4811
County	Lake

Wisconsin

Spring Bluff
Lake County
Forest Preserve

Main

WINTHROP HARBOR

Sheridan Rd.

17th St

ENTRANCE

NORTH

21st St

Shiloh Blvd

Power
House
Museum

29th St.

ZION

Power Plant

Lake Michigan

Wadsworth

ENTRANCE

MF

Hiking Trail

Sheridan Rd.

Independence Grove

Trail Length	7 miles
Surface	Paved, crushed limestone
Location & Setting	A 7 mile trail system located off Rte 137 in north Libertyville. There is both a paved and a crushed stone trail overlooking and circling a 115 acre lake. Facilities include bicycle & boat rental, water, restrooms, picnic area and a Visitors Center. Opened in 2001.
Information	Lake County Forest Preserve (847) 367-6640
County	Lake

Des Plaines River Trail

0   .25

Miles

Overlook Trail

Overlook

Des Plaines River

BRIDGE

BRIDGE

Des Plaines River Trail

North Bay

BRIDGE

North Bay Loop

Lakeside Trail

BRIDGE

Marina

River Rd.

Natural Resource Management Center

Aldler Park parking area off Milwaukee Ave. Rte. 21

137

James "Pate" Philip State Park

🚴 🛶 🚶 ⛺

Trail Length	5.0 miles
Surface	Limestone screenings
Location & Setting	The James "Pate" State Park, formerly known as the Tri-County-Trail, is located in Bartlett on the north side of Stearns Road, west of Powis Road. The park, once mainly wet, tallgrass prairie and rich with flowers and grasses, is gradually being restored to this native state. The multipurpose trails meander through some of the park's most scenic areas. The Visitor Center is open between 9 am and 5 pm Monday through Friday.
Information	Forest Preserve District of DuPage County (630) 933-7200
County	DuPage

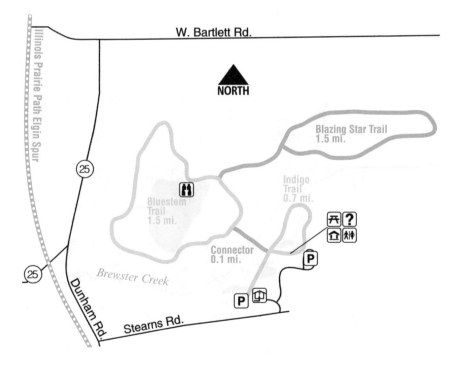

Jane Addams Trail

Trail Length	20 miles
Surface	Crushed stone
Location & Setting	The trail runs along Richland Creek between Hwy 75 in Freeport in northwestern Illinois to the Wisconsin State line and the Badger State Trail. The Badger State Trail, when completed, will connect the Jane Addams Trail to Madison, Wisconsin. The setting is rolling hills, open fields and farmland. Exposed along the trail is dolomite bedrock from an ancient shallow sea.
Information	Stephenson County Visitors Bureau (815) 233-1357
County	Stephenson

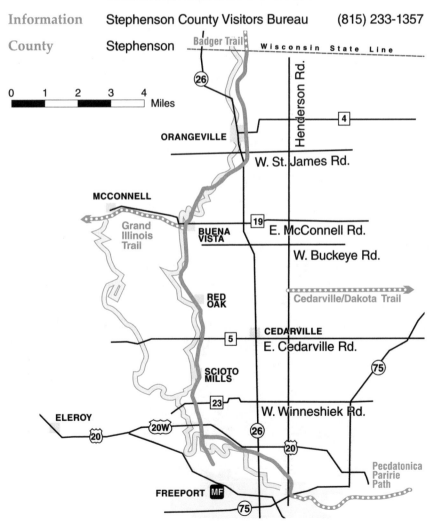

Jim Edgar Panther Creek Wildlife Area

🚲🚲🚶🎧

Trail Length & Surface	9 miles paved & 17 miles groomed for mountain biking
Location & Setting	Within the Jim Edgar Panther Creek WC is a 9 mile paved trail, a 17 mile mountain bike and hiking trail and 26 miles of hiking/equestrian trails. The Wildlife Area is located between Chandlerville and Virginia, east of the Illinois River and north of Jacksonville. The setting is Panther Creek, a 210 acre lake and its tributaries, and surrounding fields of native grass and wild flowers. The main access to the paved trail is parking lot O-11. The mountain bike trailhead is at the west lake day use area just south of Gates Road. The mountain bike trail is closed between November 1 and April 15, but remains open to hikers.
Information	Jim Edgar Panther Creek Wildlife Area (217)452-7741
County	Cass

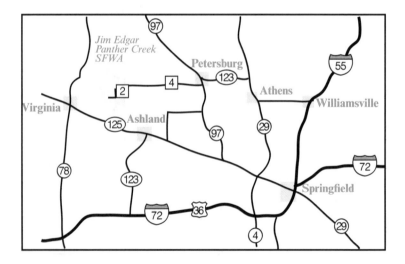

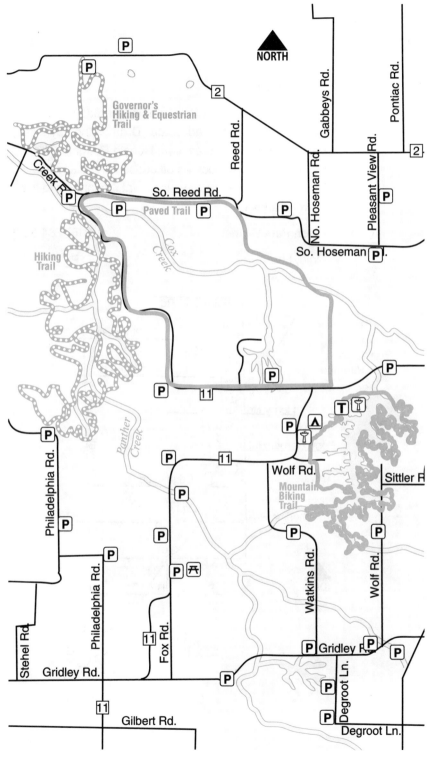

Joe Stengel Trail

Trail Length	11 miles
Surface	Gravel, Paved, Grass
Location & Setting	The trail links Dixon & Polo and was named in memory of Joe Stengel, a trail advocate. Dixon is the boyhood home of our former president, Ronald Reagan. The trailhead in Polo is located off Judson Road and in Dixon by Lowell Park, at which point it connects to the Lowell Parkway.
Information	Dixon Park District (815) 284-3306
County	Ogle, Lee

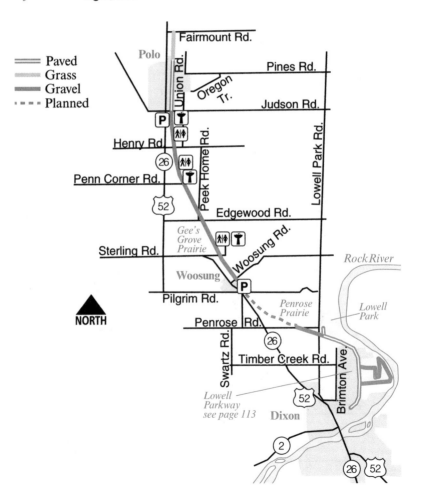

Jubilee College State Park

Trail Length	15 miles	
Surface	Natural – groomed	
Location & Setting	Jubilee College State Park is located about 10 miles northwest of Peoria between the towns of Kickapoo and Brimfield. The Park offers some 15 miles of mountain bike trails, and is open to horseback riding and snowmobiling. Setting is rolling terrain and open prairie.	
Information	Jubilee College State Park	(309) 446-3758
County	Peoria	

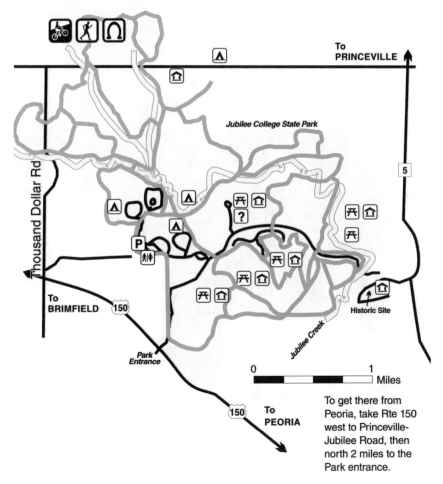

To get there from Peoria, take Rte 150 west to Princeville-Jubilee Road, then north 2 miles to the Park entrance.

Kankakee River State Park

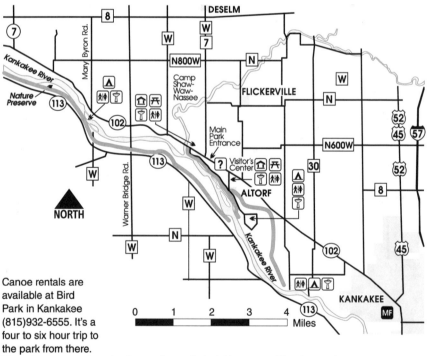

Trail Length	10.5 miles
Surface	Crushed limestone
Location & Setting	Located about 8 miles northwest of Kankakee in northeast Illinois. The park consists of some 4,000 acres with Routes 102 on the north and 113 on the south. Both I-55 and I-57 provide convenient accesses. Straddles the Kankakee River - bluffs, canyons, heavy woods. Effort level ranges from easy to difficult.
Information	Kankakee River State Park (815) 933-1383
County	Will

The bicycle trails begins at Davis Creek Area and travels to the Chippewa Campground. At one point it crosses a suspension bridge. There are 12 miles of cross country ski trails, and a 3 mile hiking trail with views of limestone canyons and a frothy waterfall. There is also a 12 mile equestrian trail.

Canoe rentals are available at Bird Park in Kankakee (815)932-6555. It's a four to six hour trip to the park from there.

There is a concession stand, camping and picnicking areas. Bicycle rentals are available (815)932-3337.

Kickapoo State Park

Trail Length	12.0 miles (loops)
Surface	Natural, groomed, single track
Location & Setting	Located in east central Illinois, 10 miles west of Indiana and 35 miles east of Champaign/Urbana. Kickapoo State Park consists of 2,842 acres and has 22 deep water ponds. The setting is made up of lushly forested uplands and bottomlands along the Middle Fork of the Vermilion River. There is easy access from I-74 and connecting roads surrounding the park.
Information	Kickapoo State Park (217) 442-4915
County	Vermilion

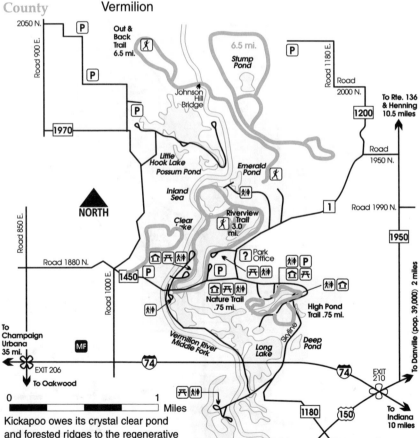

Kickapoo owes its crystal clear pond and forested ridges to the regenerative powers of nature, which reclaimed the area over the past 50 years after a century of strip mining.

Activities include hiking, canoeing, camping, horseback riding, scuba diving, in addition to bicycling.

Kishwaukee Kiwanis Pathway

Trail Length	6.5 miles
Surface	Paved
Location & Setting	The Kishwaukee Kiwanis Pathway is located in DeKalb and runs along the Kishwaukee River Between Lions Park and Hopkins Park. The setting is riverfront and open space.
Information	DeKalb Park District (815) 758-6663
County	DeKalb

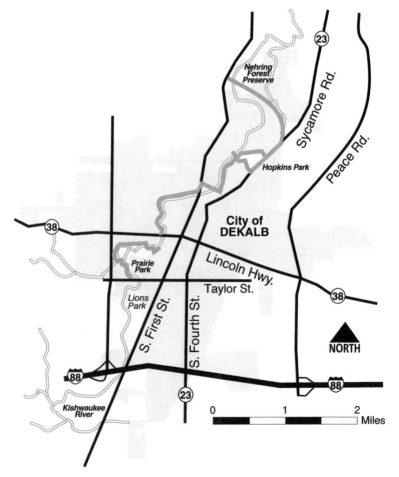

Kiwanis Trail

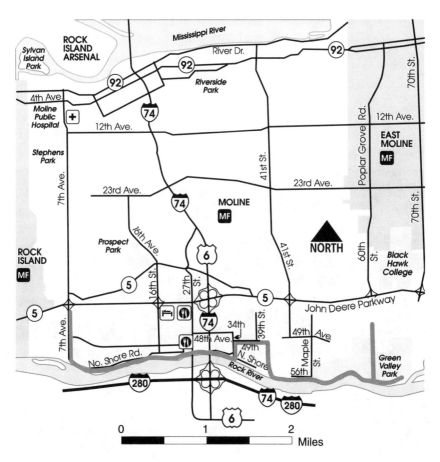

Trail Length	6.5 miles
Surface	Paved (10 feet), connecting low speed streets
Location & Setting	Located on the north side of the Rock River in Moline. It extends from 7th Street to 60th.
Information	Moline Park and Recreation Department (309) 797-0785
County	Rock Island

The trail is open from sunrise to sunset, year round. Food, lodging, sight-seeing facilities are readily available.

Lake Le-Aqua-Na State Park

Trail Length	8.5 miles
Surface	Limestone screenings, dirt.
Location & Setting	This is a beautiful 715 acre state park with a 40 acre lake and large tracts of oak, history, walnut, and pine trees. It's located near Freeport in northwest Illinois. The landscape is rolling. In addition to these trails, facilities include a small swimming beach, picnic areas, shelters and camping. The camp store is open from Memorial Day through Labor Day.

From Freeport, take Rte 20 west to IL 73 north. Take IL73 north for 2 miles into the town of Lena. Left on Lena Street for .4 miles to Lake Road, then right (north) for about 3 miles to the Park entrance. |
| **Information** | Lake Le-Aqua-Na State Park   (815)369-4282 |
| **County** | Stephenson |

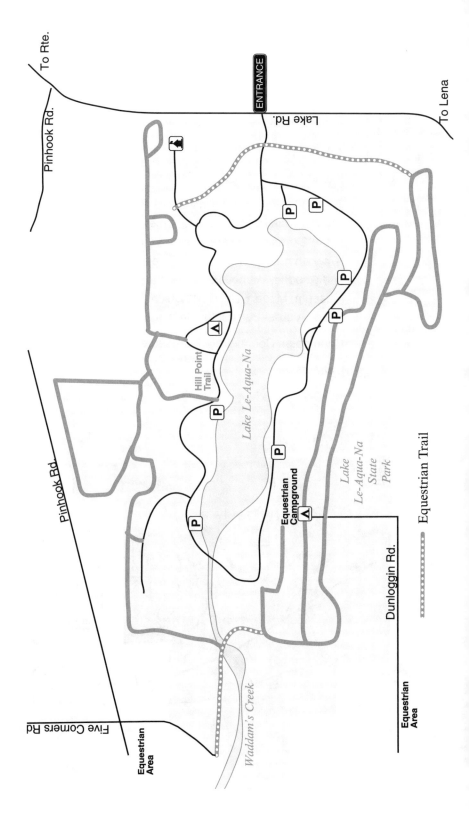

To Rte.

Pinhook Rd.

ENTRANCE

Lake Rd.

To Lena

Pinhook Rd.

Five Corners Rd

Equestrian Area

Hill Point Trail

Lake Le-Aqua-Na

Lake Le-Aqua-Na State Park

Equestrian Campground

Waddam's Creek

Dunloggin Rd.

Equestrian Area

········· Equestrian Trail

Lake of the Woods
Forest Preserve

Trail Length	4.0 miles
Surface	Paved
Location & Setting	This 900-acre preserve is located 10 miles west of Champaign-Urbana near Mahomet, along the corridor of the Sangamon River. It is easily accessible from I-74, either exit #174 or #172. The setting is rolling and wooded. Attractions include the Early American Museum, Mabery Gelvin Botanical Garden, and the Hi-Tower, a six-story structure with a bell carillon.
Information	Champaign County Forest Preserve (217) 586-3360
County	Champaign

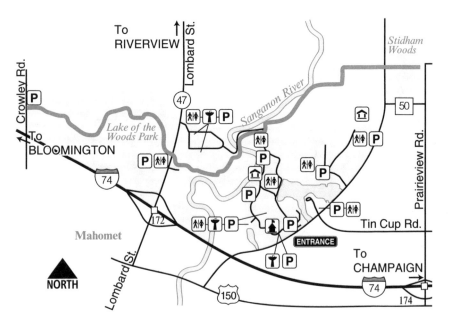

Lakewood Forest Preserve Millennium Trail

Trail Length	3 miles of the Millennium Trail
Surface	Crushed gravel
Location & Setting	Lakewood Forest Preserve is located near Wauconda, west of Mundelein and north of Lake Zurich. It is Lake County's largest preserve with 2,578-acres. The setting is rolling hills, dense oak woods, wetlands, fields, several lakes and ponds, and is home to the Lake County Discovery Museum. Lakewood also offers 9 miles of hiking trails and 6.5 miles of horse trails. The main entrance is off Route 176, just west of Fairfield Road.
Information	Lake County Forest Preserves (847) 367-6640
County	Lake

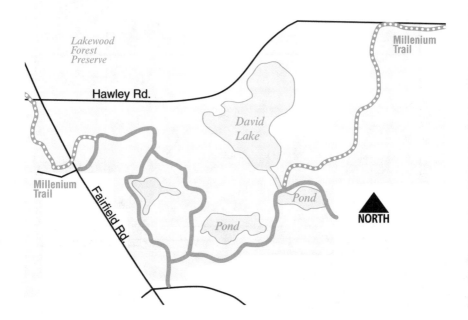

Lincoln Prairie Trail

Trail Length	15.0 miles
Surface	Asphalt
Location & Setting	The trail connects the communities of Taylorville and Pana in central Illinois, and parallels Hwy 29. It is asphalt paved, 10-feet wide, and was built on old railroad grade. Setting is rural.
Information	Office of Community Development (217) 562-3109
County	Christian

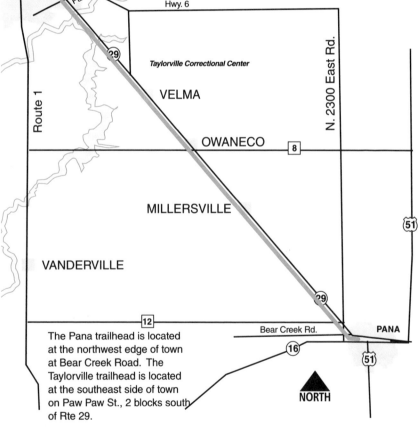

The Pana trailhead is located at the northwest edge of town at Bear Creek Road. The Taylorville trailhead is located at the southeast side of town on Paw Paw St., 2 blocks south of Rte 29.

Lost Bridge Trail

Trail Length	5.0 miles
Surface	Paved
Location & Setting	The Lost Bridge Trail, stretching from Springfield's east side to the town of Rochester, is built on an old railroad right-of-way. There is a connecting trail to Rochester Community Park, with access to parking, water and restrooms. Dense trees line each side of the trail and shields bicyclists from nearby traffic noises.
Information	Village of Rochester (217) 498-7192
County	Sangamon

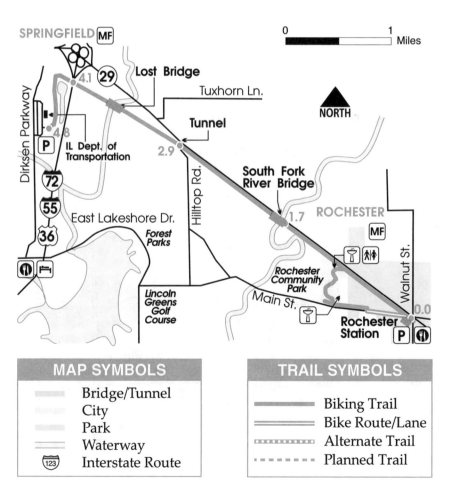

MAP SYMBOLS	
	Bridge/Tunnel
	City
	Park
	Waterway
123	Interstate Route

TRAIL SYMBOLS	
	Biking Trail
	Bike Route/Lane
	Alternate Trail
	Planned Trail

Long Prairie Trail

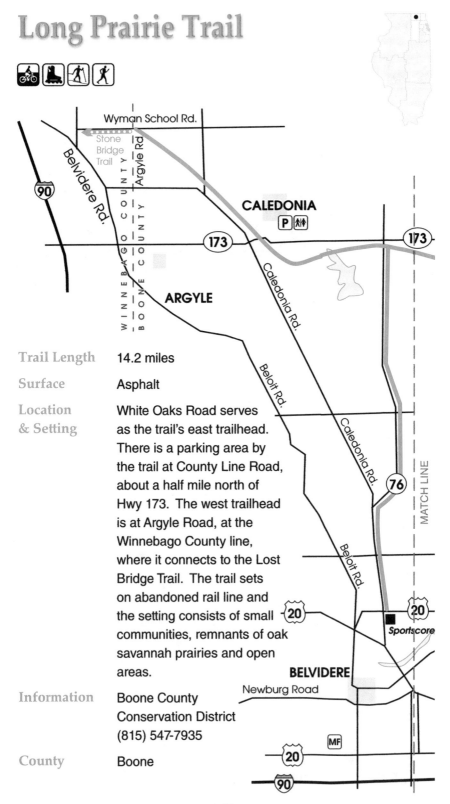

Wyman School Rd.

Stone Bridge Trail

Belvidere Rd.

90

WINNEBAGO COUNTY

Argyle Rd.

BOONE COUNTY

CALEDONIA

P

173

173

ARGYLE

Caledonia Rd.

Beloit Rd.

Caledonia Rd.

76

MATCH LINE

Beloit Rd.

20

20

Sportscore

BELVIDERE

Newburg Road

20

MF

90

Trail Length 14.2 miles

Surface Asphalt

Location & Setting White Oaks Road serves as the trail's east trailhead. There is a parking area by the trail at County Line Road, about a half mile north of Hwy 173. The west trailhead is at Argyle Road, at the Winnebago County line, where it connects to the Lost Bridge Trail. The trail sets on abandoned rail line and the setting consists of small communities, remnants of oak savannah prairies and open areas.

Information Boone County Conservation District (815) 547-7935

County Boone

There are plans to extend the trail to an area near the city of Harvard.

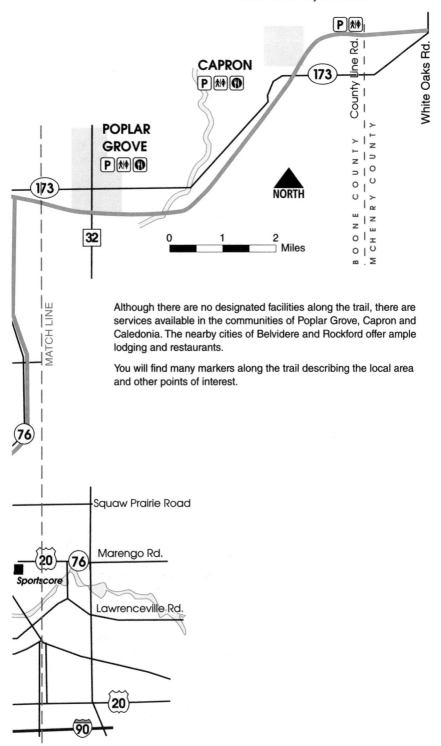

Although there are no designated facilities along the trail, there are services available in the communities of Poplar Grove, Capron and Caledonia. The nearby cities of Belvidere and Rockford offer ample lodging and restaurants.

You will find many markers along the trail describing the local area and other points of interest.

Loud Thunder
Forest Preserve

Trail Length	8.0 miles
Surface	Natural
Location & Setting	Loud Thunder has 8 miles of bi-directional single track. There are deep woods, with many climbs and downhills. Potable water is available at the horse coral during the summer. Much of the trail is marked and signed. The park closes at 10 pm. It is is located 10 miles west of Milan and 5 miles west of Andalusia, off Hwy 92. Take Hwy 92 out of the quad cities until you reach Loud Thunder Road. Take a right turn and follow signs to the horse coral. The trails are off to your left.
Information	Loud Thunder Forest Preserve (309) 795-1040
County	Rock Island

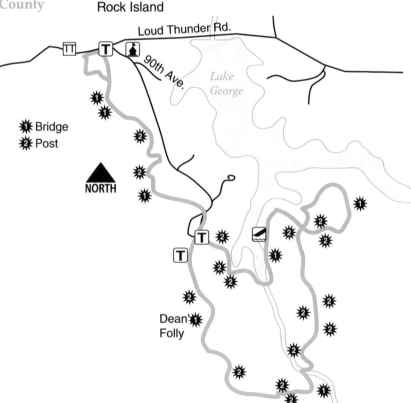

Lowell Parkway Trail

Trail Length	3.5 miles
Surface	Paved
Location & Setting	The trail is located in the town of Dixon in northwest Illinois. It begins at the Washington Avenue parking lot. There is an outhouse at its junction with the 3.5-mile gravel Meadows Trail. Other facilities include a water fountain and rest benches. Former President Ronal Reagan was a lifeguard at Lowell Park for seven seasons.
Information	Dixon Park District (815) 284-3306
County	Lee

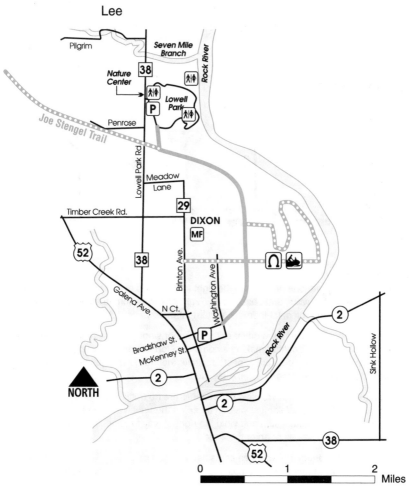

Mattoon to Charleston Trail

Trail Length	12 miles
Surface	Limestone Screenings
Location & Setting	The Mattoon to Charleston Trail is built along a ComEd right-of-way between the two cities. The surface is limestone screenings. It passes along farmland, parks, industrial areas and neighborhoods. The trail has a nice gentle grade with no significant hills.
Information	Charleston Chamber of Commerce (217) 345-7041
County	Coles

Mattoon is located in east central Illinois by Hwy 57 about 27 miles north of Hwy 70.

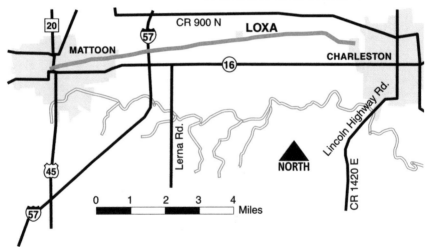

RIGHT-OF-WAY LAWS

Right-of-way means that one person has the right to go ahead of another. This applies to bicycle riders, vehicle drivers, and pedestrians. Right-of-way is something to give, not take. If others don't follow the rules, let them have the right-of-way.

At a four-way stop intersection, the driver or bicycle rider who arrives first at the intersection should be the first one to go. After making a complete stop, proceed only when it is safe to do so. Drivers and bicycle riders are expected to take their turns and go one by one through the intersection after they come to a complete stop.

At an unmarked intersection or crossing where there are no traffic signs or signals, the driver or bicycle rider on the left must yield to those on the right. When you drive out of an alley or driveway, you must stop and yield the right-of-way to pedestrians and vehicles before you cross the sidewalk or enter the street.

Emergency vehicles operating with their lights flashing and siren sounding always have the right-of-way. The law requires that you pull over to the side and stop it necessary.

McDonald Woods Forest Preserve

Trail Length 3.8 miles

Surface Limestone screenings

Location & Setting McDonald Woods is a glacial landscape of rolling hills, steep ravines and wetlands, and a great place to hike or ride your bike. You can wander through evergreen forests and meadows nestled in a valley of solitude. There are 4.5 miles of trail, of which 3.5 miles is open to biking. The granite trail loops around two large marsh ponds in a valley. The preserve is open from 6:30 am to sunset. Take Route 45 north to Grass Lake Road, then west for .7 miles to the entrance on the south side of the road.

Information Lake County Forest Preserves   (847) 369-6640

County Lake

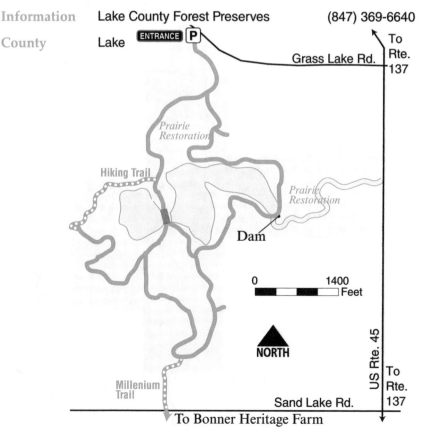

McDowell Grove Forest Preserve

Trail Length	5.6 miles	
Surface	Crushed limestone, mowed turf	
Location & Setting	This preserve is located in southwest DuPage County on Raymond Road at McDowell Avenue between Ogden Avenue and the East-West Tollway (Hwy. 88) and south of Warrenville.	
Information	Forest Preserve District of DuPage County (630) 933-7200	
County	DuPage	

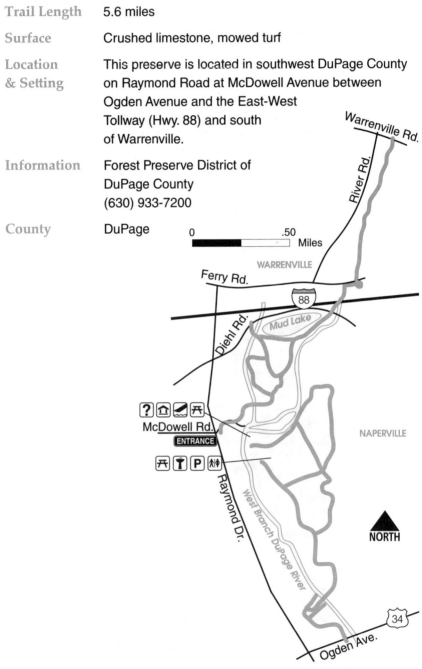

Metro East Bike Trail

Trail Length	7.5 miles
Surface	Crushed limestone
Location & Setting	This is a levee trail located near Cahokia in southwestern Illinois. The ride is flat and provides great views of the wetlands and natural areas along the Mississippi River, the St. Louis skyline, and the Cahokia Courthouse. There are no restroom or water facilities along the trail. The western trailhead access is off Hwy 10 at Cargill Elevator Road. The eastern trailhead is at Hwy 163. The trail opened in 2003.
Information	St. Clair County Highway Dept (618) 233-1392
County	St. Clair

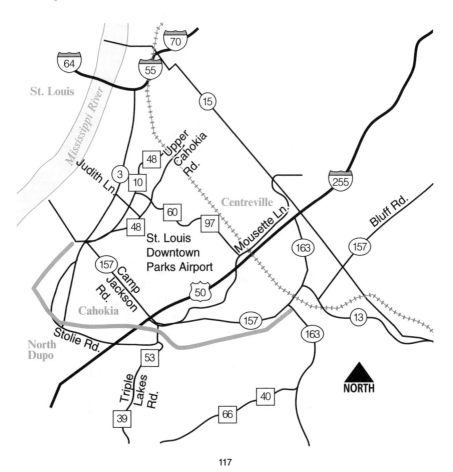

Middlefork Savanna
Forest Preserve

Trail Length	3.5 miles
Surface, Location & Setting	Crushed gravel

This 576-acre preserve is located in southeast Lake County near Lake Forest, and includes a 25-acre pocket of rare tallgrass savanna. The north branch of the Chicago River runs through it. The preserve connects to the North Shore Path at Route 176. The setting consists of scattered prairies, savannas, wetlands, and woodlands, and has been called a birder's paradise. Open hours are 6:30 am to sunset. The preserve's entrance is located near Waukegan Road and Middlefork Drive north of Route 60. Turn west on Middlefork Drive and follow signs to the parking area.

Information	Lake County Forest Preserves	(847) 367-6640
County	Lake	

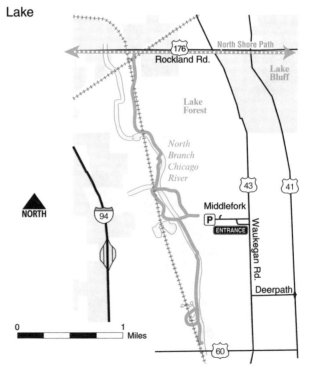

Moraine Hills State Park

🚵🏍🚶⛷🛷

Trail Length	11.6 miles
Surface	screenings – 8.9 miles; paved 1.7 miles
Location & Setting	Located 3 miles south of the city of McHenry, there is an easily recognized sign at the junction of Hwy. 176 and River Road directing you to parking. Wooded, wetlands, and is well groomed with many small hills and curves.
Information	Moraine Hills State Park (815) 385-1624
County	McHenry

Moraine Hills State Park consists of 1,690 acres. There is trail access at McHenry Dam.

Trails are one-way and color coded. There are three loops:
Lake Defiance- 3.72 miles with red markers
Leather Leaf Bog- 3.18 miles with blue markers
Fox River- 2.0 miles with yellow markers

Park hours vary with the season, but from May 1 to August 31, the park is open from 6am to 9pm.

Millenium Trail (Planned)

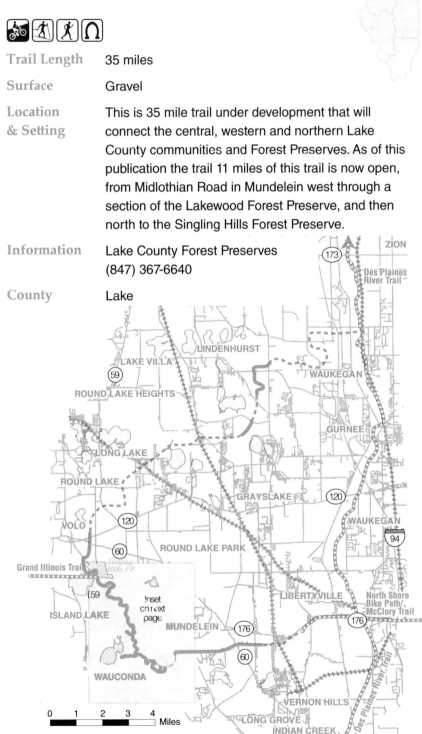

Trail Length	35 miles
Surface	Gravel
Location & Setting	This is 35 mile trail under development that will connect the central, western and northern Lake County communities and Forest Preserves. As of this publication the trail 11 miles of this trail is now open, from Midlothian Road in Mundelein west through a section of the Lakewood Forest Preserve, and then north to the Singling Hills Forest Preserve.
Information	Lake County Forest Preserves (847) 367-6640
County	Lake

ZION

173

Des Plaines River Trail

LINDENHURST

LAKE VILLA

59

WAUKEGAN

ROUND LAKE HEIGHTS

GURNEE

LONG LAKE

ROUND LAKE

GRAYSLAKE

120

VOLO

120

WAUKEGAN

94

60

ROUND LAKE PARK

Grand Illinois Trail

Singing Hills FP

59

Inset on next page

LIBERTYVILLE

North Shore Bike Path/ McClory Trail

ISLAND LAKE

MUNDELEIN

176

176

60

WAUCONDA

VERNON HILLS

Des Plaines River Trail

0 1 2 3 4 Miles

LONG GROVE

INDIAN CREEK

Millennium Trail
Hawley Street to the Singing Hills FP

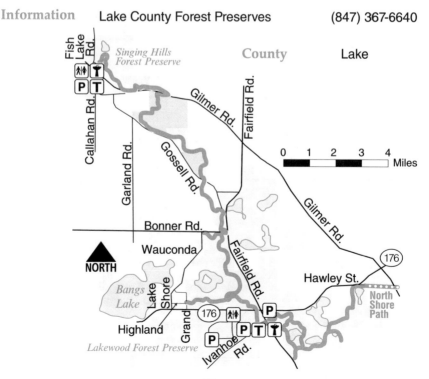

Trail Length	10 miles open	
Surface	Asphalt, crushed gravel	
Location & Setting	Completed is a 3.5-mile section from the parking area off Fairfield Road at the Lakewood FP near Wauconda east to Gilmer Read near Hawthorn Woods, a 1.1 mile section from the Singing Hills trailhead parking lot on Fish Lake Road to Gilmer Road, and a 1.5-mile section through the Liberty Lakes subdivision from Gilmer to Gossell Road. From Gossell Road there is also a 4-mile section of trail completed south to the Lakewood FP by the Shelter B parking lot on Ivanhoe Road. Under construction at the time of this printing is a 2 mile section between Wilson & Fairfield Roads, and a 1.5 mile section from Rollins Savanna FP to Hook Drive & Rollins Road.	
Information	Lake County Forest Preserves	(847) 367-6640

North Branch Bicycle Trail

Trail Length	22 miles
Surface	Paved
Location & Setting	Open spaces and wooded. The trail extends from the Chicago Botanic Gardens south for approximately 20 miles to Caldwell and Devon Avenues in Chicago. There is also an assessable parallel unpaved path that runs from a little south of Tower Road to Golf Road, and is known as the Yellow Trail.
Information	Forest Preserve District of Cook County (800) 870-3666
County	Cook

EMERGENCY ASSISTANCE

Forest Preserve
Police at
708/366-8210 or
708/366-8211

POINTS OF INTEREST	
Ⓐ	Chicago Botanic Garden
Ⓑ	Skokie Lagoons
Ⓒ	Blue Star Memorial Woods
Ⓓ	Glenview Woods
Ⓔ	Harms Woods
Ⓕ	Chick Evans Golf Course
Ⓖ	Linne Woods
Ⓗ	Miami Woods
Ⓘ	Clayton Smith Woods
Ⓙ	Whealan Pool
Ⓚ	Edgebrook Golf Course
Ⓛ	Billy Caldwell Golf Course

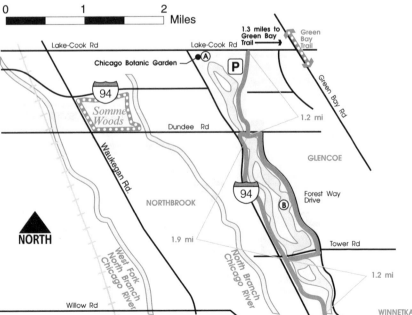

The trail winds along the North Branch of the Chicago River and the Skokie Lagoons, providing access to various picnic groves and communities in addition to the Botanic Gardens.

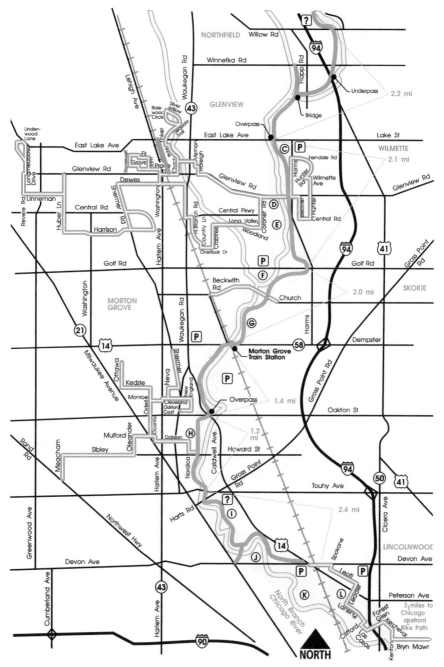

North Shore Path

Trail Length	8.5 miles
Surface	Limestone screenings, paved
Location & Setting	Proceeds west from just south of Rockland Rd. (Hwy. 176) in Lake Bluff to Hwy. 45 in Mundelein. Surburban, open and lightly wooded areas.
Information	Lake County Dept. of Transportation (847) 362-3950
County	Lake

131
14th St
NORTH MF
41
CHICAGO
22nd St
M.L. King Dr.
Sheridan Rd.
LAKE MICHIGAN

0   1   2   Miles

137
137
94
Des Plaines
River Trail
Skokie Hwy.
Green Bay Rd
Robert
McClory
Bike
Path
21
NORTH
Butterfield Rd.
LIBERTYVILLE
MF
LAKE
BLUFF
176
Rockland Rd
MF
176
MF
45
Underpass
131
LAKE
FOREST
41
Carmel High School
Des Plaines River
MUNDELEIN MF
Des Plaines
River Trail
Robert McClory
Bike Path

TRAIL SYMBOLS

━━━━━	Biking Trail
═════	Bike Route/Lane
▭▭▭▭▭	Alternate Trail
▪ ▪ ▪ ▪	Planned Trail
++++++++++	Railroad Tracks

Oakhurst Forest Preserve

Trail Length	10 miles
Surface	Paved and gravel
Location & Setting	Oakhurst is located in Aurora, on Fifth Avenue, about a ½-mile east of Farnsworth Avenue. This preserve contains a 55-acre lake/marsh complex, called Lake Patterson, with excellent opportunities for wildlife observation. The silt-laden canary grass wetland has been restored to a high quality marsh. There are also two 20-acre woodlands with a full complement of understory and native flora.
Information	Kane County Forest Preserves (630) 232-5980
County	Kane

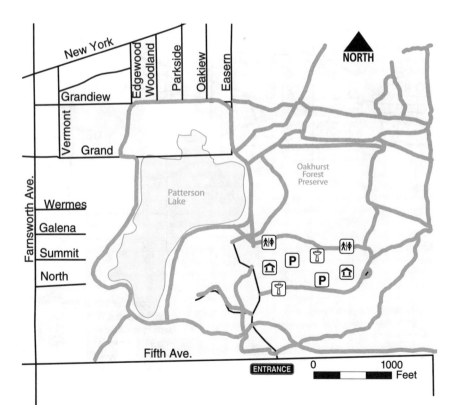

Old Plank Road Trail

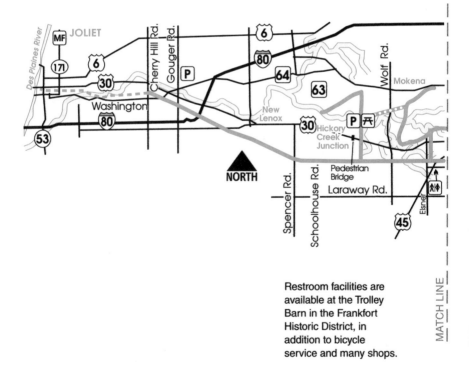

Trail Length	21 miles	
Surface	Asphalt	
Location & Setting	Located in Cook and Will Counties, the trail will become a major link in the Grand Illinois Trail. It extends from Western Avenue in Park Forest to Cherry Hill Road east of Joliet. Plans include its extension to the I & M Canal State Trail. Hickory Creek Junction, a half mile north of the trail, serves as an access point with parking and a pedestrian bridge over Highway 30. The setting is urban with open and some wooded areas.	
Information	Will County Forest Preserve	(815) 727-8700
County	Cook, Will	

Restroom facilities are available at the Trolley Barn in the Frankfort Historic District, in addition to bicycle service and many shops.

RULES OF THE TRAIL

Hours of operation are from dawn
to dusk

No alcoholic beverages

No motorized vehicles

No camping or fires

Stay on the trail

Picking or damaging plants on the
trail is prohibited

Obey all posted signs

TRAIL SYMBOLS	
▬▬▬▬▬	Biking Trail
══════	Bike Route/Lane
▭▭▭▭▭	Alternate Trail
▪ ▪ ▪ ▪ ▪ ▪	Planned Trail
┼┼┼┼┼┼┼┼┼	Railroad Tracks

The METRA station, located between Park Forest and Matteson, provides transportation to the Chicago Loop. There is parking, bike racks and lockers at the Park Forest municipal parking lot.

From the eastern trailhead, the Sauk Trail Woods is located a half mile to the east. Plans are to acquire a railroad right-of-way in Chicago Heights to connect these trails.

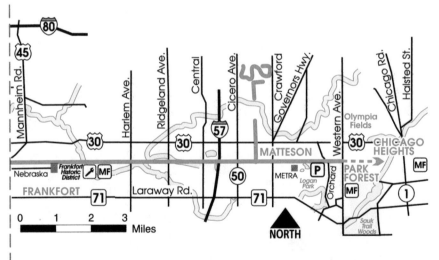

Logan Park, between Orchard Drive and Crawford Avenue, is a point from which to access the trail. Parking is available just south of the trail.

Old School Forest Preserve

Trail Length	6.0 miles
Surface	1.5 miles paved, 4.5 miles crushed gravel
Location & Setting	Old School is one of Lake County's most popular preserves. Its trails connect to the Des Plaines River Trail. Activities include picnicking, fishing, a playground, and a sled hill. Large oaks dominate these woodlands, which are interspersed with small prairies.
Information	Lake County Forest Preserves (847) 367-6640
County	Lake

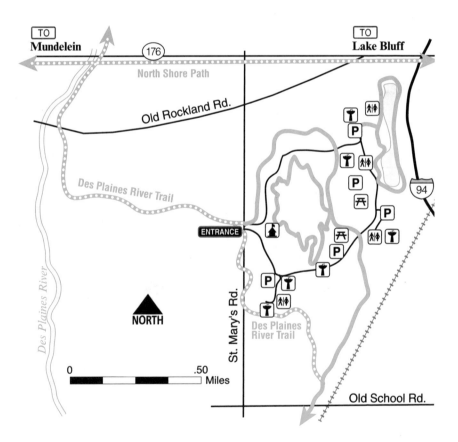

Peace Road Trail

Trail Length	10 miles
Surface	Screenings
Location & Setting	The Peace Road Trail extends from Bethany Road in Sycamore to Pleasant Street in DeKalb. Current access to the Great Western Trail is by way of Airport Road. The setting is rural with farmland, woods and open areas.
Information	DeKalb County Forest Preserve (815) 527-4005
County	DeKalb

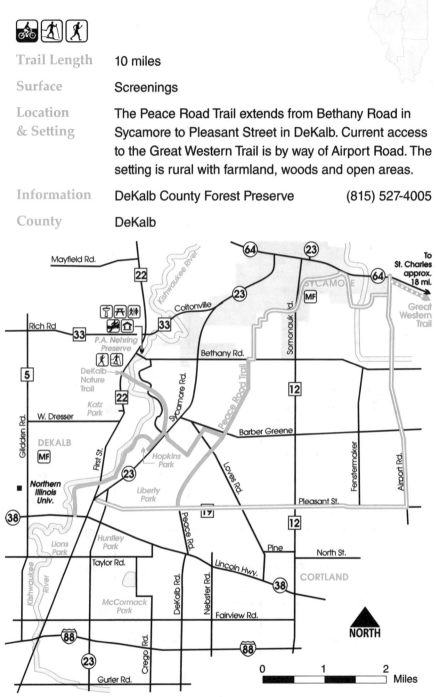

Planned construction includes a path between the Peace Road Trail and both Hopkins Park and the DeKalb Nature Trail. Also planned is an alternate route connecting to the Great Western Trail.

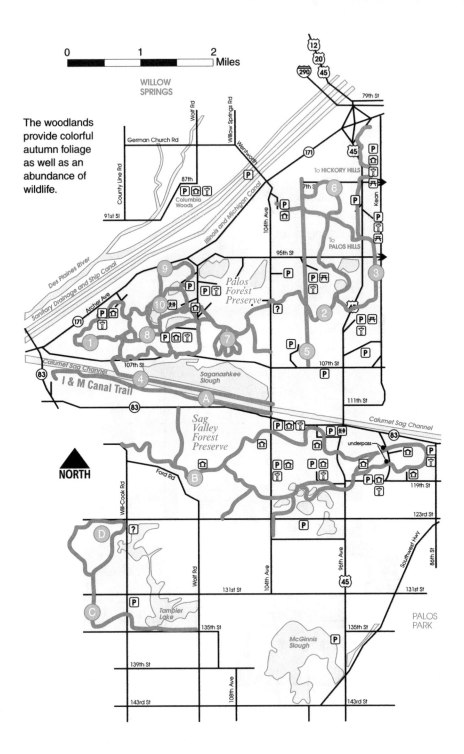

The woodlands provide colorful autumn foliage as well as an abundance of wildlife.

A suggested trail access is by 104th St. (Willow Springs Avenue) and Hwy. 171 (Archer Ave.)

Palos Forest Preserve
Sag Valley Forest Preserve
I&M Canal Trail (Cook County)

Trail Length & Surface	Palos – approximately 25 miles; natural, groomed Sag – 10.5 miles; natural, groomed I&M Canal Trail (Cook County) – 9 miles; paved	

Location & Setting	Located in southwestern Cook County, Palos and Sag together encompass more than 15,000 acres of woods, prairie, and wetlands in a hilly triangle. Two deep valleys slice between two high mounds of glacial debris, known as moraines, with forested hills rising 159-feet above the flat prairie stretching toward Lake Michigan. The woodlands provide colorful autumn foliage as well as an abundance of wildlife. The I&M Canal Trail area is open and flat.
	To reach the complex, you can exit south from I-55 on Route 45 (LaGrange Road) and drive about two miles. A suggested trail access is by 104th Street (Willow Springs Avenue) and Hwy 171 (Archer Avenue). There is a parking lot with a paved trail running through it. Nearby is a visitor's center that explains the history of the National Heritage Corridor.
Information	Forest Preserve District of Cook County (800) 870-3666
County	Cook

Palos Trail Names & Mileage			Sag Trail Names & Mileage		
1	Orange Trail Loop	5.6 mi	A	Purple Trail	3.2 mi
2	Yellow Trail	5.2 mi	B	Green Trail	2.0 mi
3	Brown Trail (east)	3.8 mi	C	Red Trail	2.4 mi
4	Blue Trail (south)	2.6 mi	D	Brown Trail	2.9 mi
5	Tan Trail	2.5 mi			
6	Red Trail	1.5 mi			
7	Black Trail	1.4 mi			
8	Brown Trail (west)	1.5 mi			
9	Blue Trail (north)	1.2 mi			
10	Green Trail (west)	1.0 mi			

Pecatonica Prairie Path

Trail Length	18 miles
Surface	Ballast, grass & dirt
Location & Setting	The trail follows an old railroad right-of-way through Stephenson and Winnebago counties. The eastern trailhead is off Meridian Road just south of Hwy. 20 and west of the city of Rockford. The western trailhead is south of the intersection of Hillcrest Road and River Road, off Hwy. 75, 3 miles east of Freeport. The trails pass through open areas and farmland. Lightly wooded.
Information	Pecatonica Village Hall (815) 239-2310
County	Winnebago, Stephenson

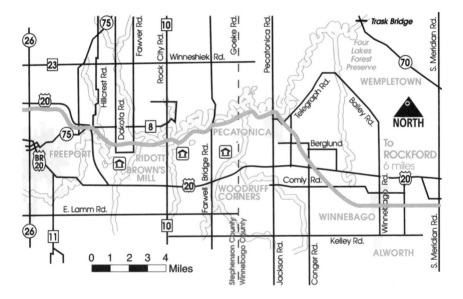

A variety of animals, birds and native wild flowers can be found along the corridor. The right-of-way is owned by Commonwealth Edison, which leases it to Pecatonica Prairie Path, Inc.

Perryville Bike Path

Trail Length	9 miles
Surface	Paved
Location & Setting	The Perryville Path is located in Rockford on the east side of Perryville Road from Hart Road south to Spring Brook Road, where it crosses to the west side. From Spring Brook Road south to Argus Drive the Bike path is located on the west side of Perryville Road. There is a 1.4-mile loop at Midway Village & Museum Center, and a 2.4–mile loop through Rock Valley College. There are plans to extend the trail system. The setting is urban.
Information	Rockford Park District (815)-987-8800
County	Winnebago

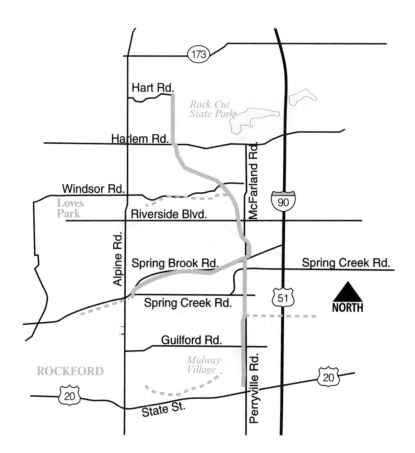

Pimiteoui Trail

Trail Length	Approximately 5 miles
Surface	Paved
Location & Setting	Located in the city of Peoria, south to north, from the Robert Mitchell Bridge to the Pioneer Parkway. Urban and open areas.
Information	Peoria Park District (309) 682-6684
County	Peoria

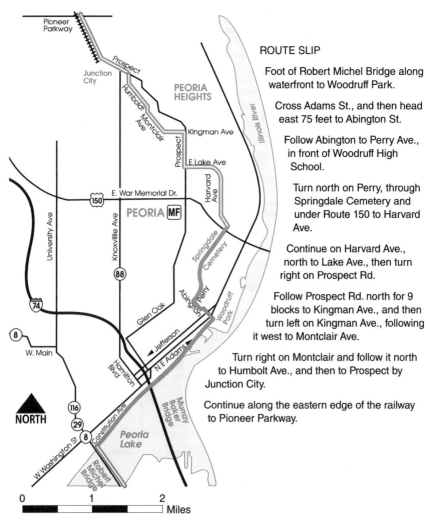

ROUTE SLIP

Foot of Robert Michel Bridge along waterfront to Woodruff Park.

Cross Adams St., and then head east 75 feet to Abington St.

Follow Abington to Perry Ave., in front of Woodruff High School.

Turn north on Perry, through Springdale Cemetery and under Route 150 to Harvard Ave.

Continue on Harvard Ave., north to Lake Ave., then turn right on Prospect Rd.

Follow Prospect Rd. north for 9 blocks to Kingman Ave., and then turn left on Kingman Ave., following it west to Montclair Ave.

Turn right on Montclair and follow it north to Humbolt Ave., and then to Prospect by Junction City.

Continue along the eastern edge of the railway to Pioneer Parkway.

Poplar Creek Forest Preserve

Trail Length	15.2 miles
Surface	Paved, dirt single track
Location & Setting	The 4,500 acre Poplar Creek Forest Preserve is located in northwest Cook County, bordered by Hoffman Estates to the east, west and south, and South Barrington to the north. Wooded, with access to toilets, water and picnic facilities. Portions of the Preserve have been restored to original Illinois prairie. The entrance is on the west side of Barrington Road, south of W. Higgins Road and the Northwest Tollway. In addition to the paved trail, there are several miles of dirt single-track west of Route 59. They can be reached by following the grass path heading southwest from the intersection at Route 58/59, or from the back of the picnic area off Route 59.
Information	Cook County Forest Preserve District (800) 870-3666
County	Cook

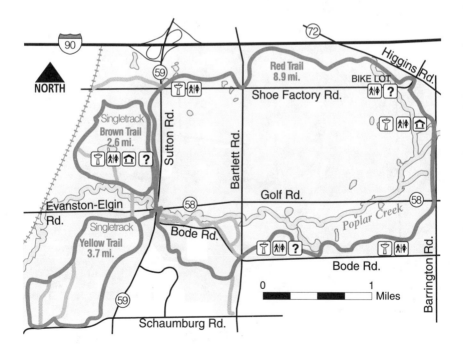

Potawatomi Trail–McNaughton Park

Trail Length	15.0 miles
Surface	Natural – groomed
Location & Setting	The Powawatomi Trail is located in Pekin at McNaughton Park. The trail begins and ends at the Totem Pole, behind the stables, and is also open to hiking and horseback riding. Red markers indicate the main trail. The park covers some 850-acres of beautiful woodland and meadows.
Information	Pekin Park District Recreation Department (309) 347-7275
County	Tazewell

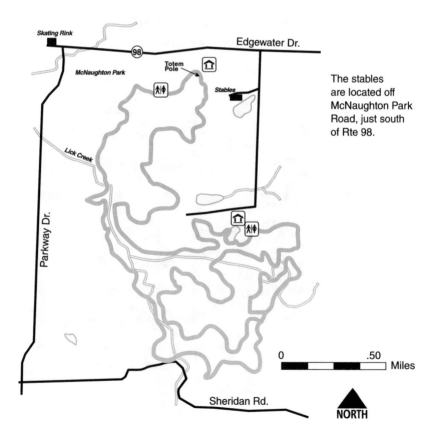

The stables are located off McNaughton Park Road, just south of Rte 98.

Pratts Wayne Woods
Forest Preserve

🚵 🚵 🎿 🚶 🔦 👟

Trail Length	8.7 miles
Surface	Asphalt, limestone screenings, mowed turf
Location & Setting	Located in the northwest corner of DuPage County between Wayne and Barlett. Access from Powis Road a mile north of Army Trail Road or from the Illinois Prairie Path. It's 2,600 acres include savannas, marshes, meadows and prairies. Wildlife and plants abound.
Information	Forest Preserve District of DuPage County (630) 933-7200
County	DuPage

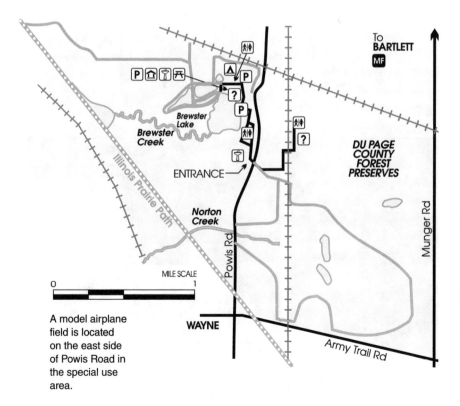

A model airplane field is located on the east side of Powis Road in the special use area.

Prairie Trail

Trail Length   26.0 miles

Surface   Paved from Algonquin to Ringwood, ballast & gravel from Ringwood to the Wisconsin border

Location & Setting   From Algonquin north to the Wisconsin State Line. Open space, wooded areas, small communities.

Information   McHenry County Conservation District   (815) 338-6223

County   McHenry

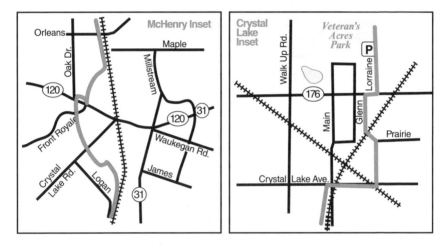

Richmond is an interesting small community with several antique shops. The trail crosses Hwy. 173 just west of Hwy. 31. There is no designated parking.

Fat tires are recommended as the trail is somewhat rough from equestrian use.

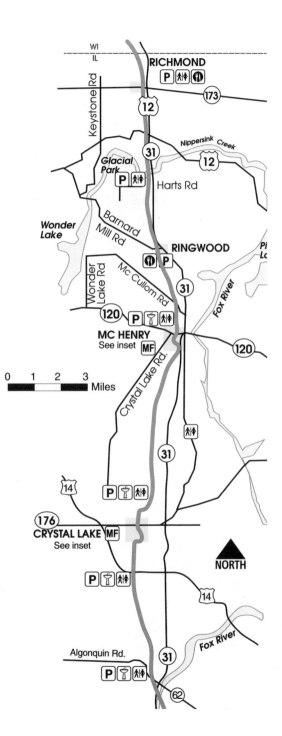

Pyramid State Park

Trail Length 16.5 miles

Surface Natural – groomed

Location & Setting Pyramid State Park, with 19,701 acres, consists of heavily forested hills with many lakes and ponds. It is located about 5 miles south of Pinckneyville, off Routes 127/13 in southern Illinois. The surface is dirt and generally flat with some hills. Tent and trail camping is available, with both Class C & D campsites. Canoeing is popular.

Information Pyramid State Park   (618) 357-2574

County Perry

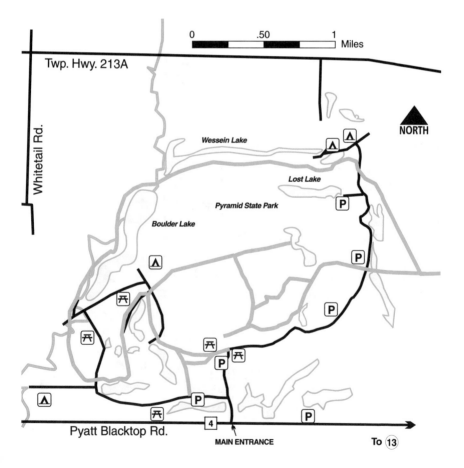

Raven Glen Forest Preserve

Trail Length	4.1 miles
Surface	Crushed gravel
Location & Setting	Located in north-central Lake County, the 544-acre Raven Glen FP is a blend of former agricultural and recreational lands. The setting consists of gently rolling hills, scenic vistas, a grove of oaks and hickories, and the 33-acre Timber Lake. Facilities include picnic tables, benches, an overlook, comfort station, water pump and a horse trailer parking area.
Information	Lake County Forest Preserves (847) 367-6640
County	Lake

Red Hills State Park

Trail Length	8 miles
Surface	Screenings, natural
Location & Setting	Located in southeastern Illinois between Olney and Lawrence-ville on U.S. Route 50. The park consists of 948 acres with wooded hills, deep ravines, meadows and year round springs.
Information	Red Hills State Park (618) 936-2469
County	Lawrence

Old Settler Day is a popular weekend event usually scheduled late in April. Red Hill is the highest point of land between St. Louis and Cincinnati. It has a 120 foot tower and cross rising from its summit.

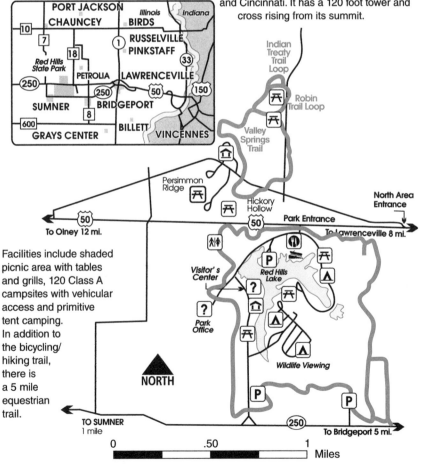

Facilities include shaded picnic area with tables and grills, 120 Class A campsites with vehicular access and primitive tent camping. In addition to the bicycling/ hiking trail, there is a 5 mile equestrian trail.

Rend Lake Biking Trails

Trail Length	9.8 miles
Surface	Paved
Location & Setting	The current 9.8 miles of trail are located on the east side of Rend Lake, and consist of the 6-mile trail running through Wayne Fitzgerrlll State Park, and the 3.8 mile Gun Creek Trail that runs from the Visitor Center to the North Marcum Swim Beach. The trails are not connected. Additional trail is under development on the south end of the lake. The trails are paved, and bike rentals are available. Rend Lake is located just north of Benton on Rte 154. There are numerous access points.
Information	Rend Lake Visitors Center (618) 439-7430
County	Jefferson, Franklin

SESSER

Coal St.

Peach Orchard Rd.

Rend City Rd.

NORTH

57

Wayne Fitzgerrell State Park

WHITINGTON

154

148

Rend Lake

DuQuoin St.

Central St.

57

37

14

BENTON
WEST CITY

River Trail of Illinois

Trail Length	10.8 miles
Surface	Paved, limestone screenings
Location & Setting	This 10-foot wide trail runs between Morton and East Peoria along the old Illinois Terminal Railway line between Peoria and Bloomington. The setting includes tallgrass prairie, bluffs and forest habitats. Facilities include a Visitors Center, restrooms and picnic facilities.
Information	Fon du Lac Park District (309) 699-3923
County	Tazewell

Western Access: Southern end of Robert Michel Bridge by the Embassy Suites. A short section south of the bridge to the levee has not yet been completed.

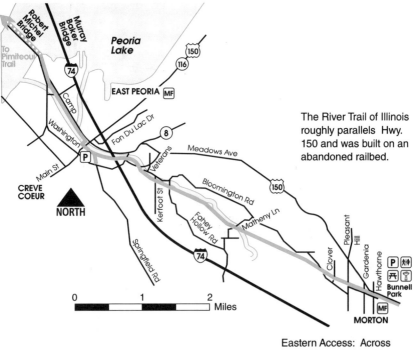

The River Trail of Illinois roughly parallels Hwy. 150 and was built on an abandoned railbed.

Eastern Access: Across from K-Mart and La Fiesta Mexican Restaurant.

TRAIL SYMBOLS

▬▬▬▬	Biking Trail
═══════	Bike Route/Lane
▭▭▭▭▭	Alternate Trail
▬ ▬ ▬ ▬	Planned Trail
+++++++++	Railroad Tracks

TRAIL USES

🚲 Bicycling

🚵 Mountain Bicycling

🚶 Hiking

⛷ Cross-Country Skiing

🛼 Inline Skating

🏔 Snowmobiling

🎠 Bridal Path

FACILITIES

🏊 Beach/Swimming

🚲 Bicycle Repair

🏠 Cabin

▲ Camping

🛶 Canoe Launch

✚ First Aid

🍴 Food

GC Golf Course

? Information

🛏 Lodging

MF Multi-Facilities

P Parking

🏕 Picnic

🚒 Ranger Station

🚻 Restrooms

🏠 Shelter

T Trailhead

🏛 Visitor/Nature Center

🚰 Water

🔭 Overlook/Observation

Robert McClory Bike Path

Trail Length	25 miles
Surface	Limestone screenings, paved
Uses	Leisure bicycling, cross country skiing, hiking/jogging
Location & Setting	The trail runs north and south from the Cook County line (Lake Cook Road) to the Wisconsin border. The setting is surburban, open and lightly wooded areas.
Information	Lake County Dept. of Transportation (847) 562-3950
County	Lake

Some of the surface is limestone screenings. The remainder is paved, or street/sidewalk connections.

Screenings:

Highland Park
- Ravinia Park to Laurel (2 mi.)

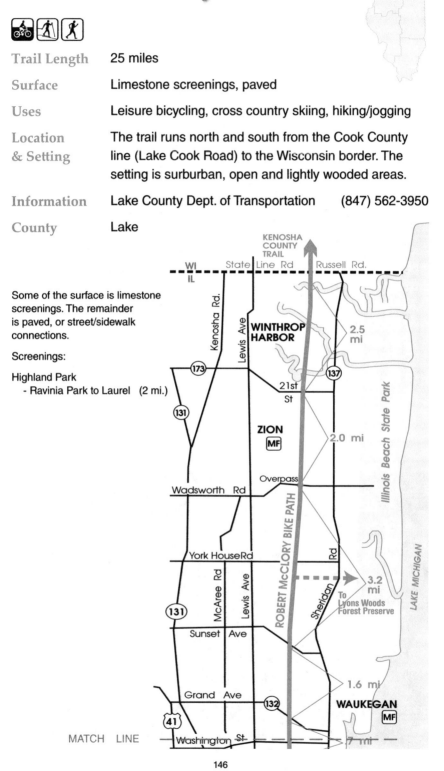

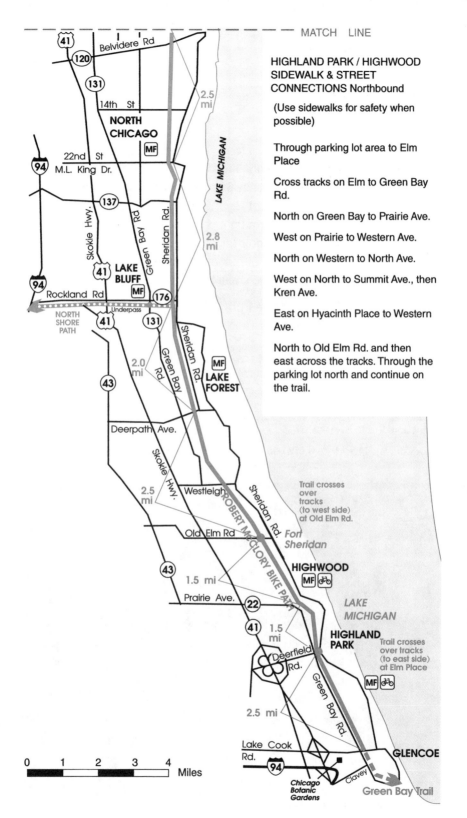

HIGHLAND PARK / HIGHWOOD SIDEWALK & STREET CONNECTIONS Northbound

(Use sidewalks for safety when possible)

Through parking lot area to Elm Place

Cross tracks on Elm to Green Bay Rd.

North on Green Bay to Prairie Ave.

West on Prairie to Western Ave.

North on Western to North Ave.

West on North to Summit Ave., then Kren Ave.

East on Hyacinth Place to Western Ave.

North to Old Elm Rd. and then east across the tracks. Through the parking lot north and continue on the trail.

NORTH CHICAGO

LAKE MICHIGAN

2.5 mi

2.8 mi

LAKE BLUFF

NORTH SHORE PATH

Underpass

2.0 mi

LAKE FOREST

Deerpath Ave.

Westleigh

ROBERT McCLORY BIKE PATH

2.5 mi

Old Elm Rd

Trail crosses over tracks (to west side) at Old Elm Rd.

Fort Sheridan

HIGHWOOD

Prairie Ave.

1.5 mi

1.5 mi

Deerfield Rd.

LAKE MICHIGAN

HIGHLAND PARK

Trail crosses over tracks (to east side) at Elm Place

2.5 mi

Green Bay Rd.

GLENCOE

Lake Cook Rd.

Chicago Botanic Gardens

Clavey

Green Bay Trail

0 1 2 3 4 Miles

Belvidere Rd

14th St

22nd St
M.L. King Dr.

Rockland Rd

Skokie Hwy.

Green Bay Rd.

Sheridan Rd.

Skokie Hwy.

Sheridan Rd.

Rock Cut State Park

Trail Length	23 miles
Surface	Dirt
Location & Setting	Located in Winnebago County northeast of Rockford, and approximately 80 miles northwest of Chicago. From I-90, exit at East Riverside Blvd. and head west for 1 mile, then turn right on McFarland Road to Harlem Road (dead end). Turn east (right) for a little over a mile, over I-90, to the Park entrance. Terrain is rugged, rocky with woods and small hills.
Information	Rock Cut State Park (815) 885-3311
	Emergency 911
County	Winnebago

The trails are identified by colored trail markers. Blue Trails are for mountain biking and hiking, yellow trails are for equestrian and hiking, and red trails are restricted to hiking only. Mountain biking and equestrian trails are open April 1st to November 30th. The track varies from 5 to 10 feet wide.

Rock Cut State Park consists of 3,096 acres. Facilities include concessions, restrooms, water, camping, boat rental, and canoe access.

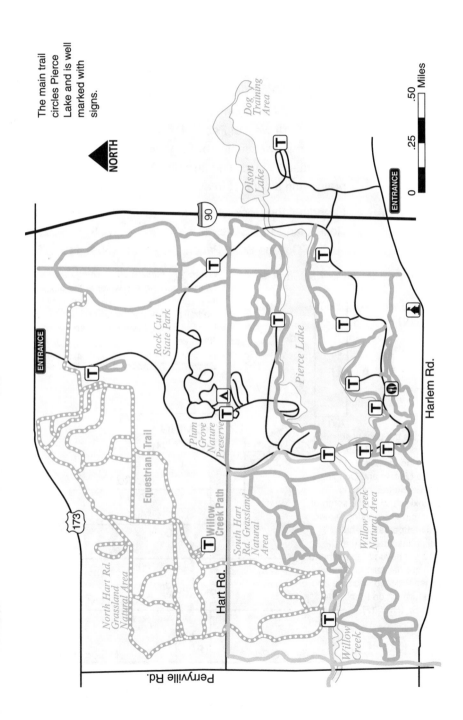

The main trail circles Pierce Lake and is well marked with signs.

NORTH

90

173

ENTRANCE

ENTRANCE

Perryville Rd.

Hart Rd.

Harlem Rd.

North Hart Rd. Grassland Natural Area

Equestrian Trail

Rock Cut State Park

Plum Grove Nature Preserve

Willow Creek Path

South Hart Rd. Grassland Natural Area

Willow Creek Natural Area

Willow Creek

Pierce Lake

Olson Lake

Dog Training Area

0   .25   .50   Miles

Rock Island State Trail

Trail Length   28.3 miles

Surface   Limestone screenings

Location & Setting   Stretches from Pioneer Parkway along an old railroad right-of-way through the communities of Dunlap, Princeville, and Wyoming to the edge of Toulon in Stark County northwest of Peoria. The trail lies in a vast plain formerly occupied by tallgrass prairie. The land is dominated by cultivated fields but numerous patches of prairie and stands of trees are scattered along the route.

Information

Friends of the Rock Island Trail	(309) 266-5085
Rock Island Trail State Park	(309) 695-2228
Jubilee College State Park	(309) 446-3758

County   Peoria, Stark

Wyoming – Once a coal mining area. There is parking and water at the old train station along the trail. Connect with the trail northbound by taking Hwy. 17 to Thomas St. for 1 block and then right onto 6th Street.

```
0     1     2     3     4
                              Miles
```

91 **17** **TOULON**

800 E   900 E

P Spoon River

750 N

Toulon is the county seat of Stark County. There is a courthouse built in 1856 where Lincoln and Douglas spoke. The trail head is approximately 1 mile south of town and has parking, water, and restrooms. To enter Toulon take the road to the right just beyond the trailhead for a quarter mile to Clinton Street. Proceed one mile and then turn left on Franklin to Main St. (Hwy. 17).

17 **91**

6th St

17

WYOMING

P

Twp Rd 135

500 N

N Valley Rd

400 N

W. Jersey Rd

300 N

Camp Run Creek

91   County Hwy 3

150 N

Spoon River

STARK COUNTY
PEORIA COUNTY

County Line Rd

P

Mud Run Creek

N Cedar Bluff Rd

Streitmatter Rd

MATCH LINE

Other features of The Rock Island Trail include:
An arched culvert with wing wall construction of massive limestone blocks, located about 2 miles north of Alta. A steel trestle bridge, circa 1910, spanning the Spoon River. A rehabilitated rail station in Wyoming, which was built in 1871.

PRINCEVILLE You cross the Santa Fe railroad tracks as you enter the town from the south. Just beyond the tracks is a park with restrooms and a picnic area. The trail connects through city streets- proceed on Walnut to North Ave. a short distance and left onto North Town Rd. for a half mile. Turn left on a marked single lane road to connect with the trail again.

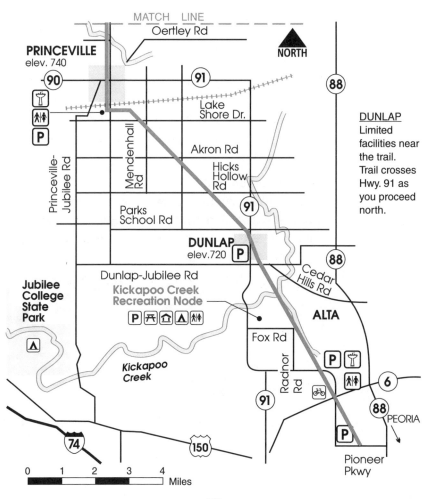

DUNLAP
Limited facilities near the trail. Trail crosses Hwy. 91 as you proceed north.

Rock Run Trail
Joliet Junction Trail

🚲🥾🚶⛸️

Trail Length & Surface	Rock Run	9 miles, paved & crushed limestone
	Joliet Junction	4.4 miles, paved

Location & Setting

Rock Run Trail

The trail can be accessed from the I&M Canal by way of Empress Road (Houbolt Avenue), a ¼-mile south of I-80 in Joliet. The trail follows Houbolt Avenue for 0.8 miles to the Joliet Junior College campus where it skirts around the college and continues northward for 2.8 miles to McDonough. A 0.5-mile spur connects the trail to Jefferson Street. The Black Road Access is located on Black Road, approximately a ¼-mile east of the I-55 overpass in Joliet. The trail connects to the Paul V. Nickols access at Essington and Ingalls Avenues. The preserve is open from dawn to dusk. There is an observation deck that offers a scenic view of a pond and Rock Run Creek. Facilities include restrooms, water, picnic areas, and a pavilion surrounded by restored tallgrass prairie.

Joliet Junction Trail

The trail runs from Larkin Street to Theodore Street, which is just south of Crest Hill and Hwy 30. It connects with the I&M Canal Trail from Larkin Street, and to Rock Run Trail at Theodore Street.

Information	Forest Preserve District of Will County	(815) 727-8700
County	Will	

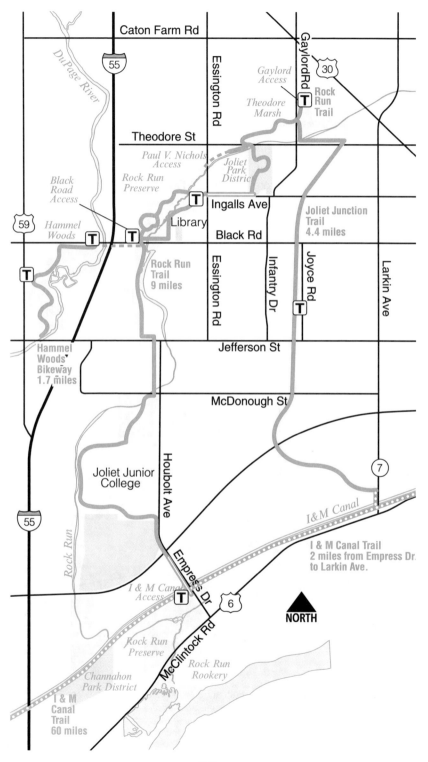

Caton Farm Rd

55

DuPage River

Essington Rd

Gaylord Rd

30

Gaylord Access

Rock Run Trail

Theodore Marsh

Theodore St

Paul V. Nichols Access

Joliet Park District

Black Road Access

Rock Run Preserve

T Ingalls Ave

Library

Joliet Junction Trail 4.4 miles

59

Hammel Woods

T

T

Black Rd

Rock Run Trail 9 miles

Essington Rd

Infantry Dr

Joyce Rd

T

Larkin Ave

Hammel Woods Bikeway 1.7 miles

Jefferson St

McDonough St

Joliet Junior College

Houbolt Ave

55

Rock Run

I & M Canal

7

I & M Canal Trail 2 miles from Empress Dr. to Larkin Ave.

Empress Dr

I & M Canal Access

T

6

NORTH

McClintock Rd

Rock Run Preserve

Rock Run Rookery

Channahon Park District

I & M Canal Trail 60 miles

Rock River & Sportscore Recreation Path

Trail Length	8.0 miles	
Surface	Asphalt	
Location & Setting	The path follows the Rock River in Rockford from Walnut Street north through Veterans Memorial Park/ Sportscore to Harlem Road. The setting is urban.	
Information	Rockford Park District	(815) 987-8800
County	Winnebago	

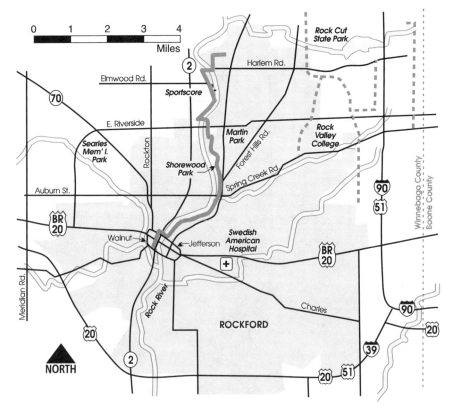

The Sportscore joins the Rock River Path at Elmwood Road, proceeds along Brown Beach Road jogging west, then northeast along Harlem Road and across the Rock River. The path crosses the Rock River at Jefferson Street, Riverside Blvd. and Harlem Road. There are numerous points of interest along the path.

Rock Run Greenway

Trail Length
3.0 miles

Surface
Asphalt

Location & Setting
This 3 mile asphalt paved trail is located in Will County. The Preserve, once wetland, is now being restored. It extends from 1.5 miles from Theodore Marsh on Theodore Street in Crest Hill south and west. From there it loops through to Black Road for 1.4 miles. Pick up the trail again at Jefferson for another 4 miles to the I&M Canal Access, and Joliet Junior College. Open hours are from 8 am to 8 pm. There is an entrance on the west side of Essington Road at Ingalls Avenue, and off the north side of Black Road west of Essington Road.

Information
Forest Preserve District of Will County   (815) 727-8700

County
Will

Rock Run Trail
.65 mi.

Prairie Trail
.25 mi.

Wetland Trail
.75 mi.

Sedge Meadow Trail
.25 mi.

Paul V. Nichols Access

Essington Rd.

Rock Run

1.0 mi. library spur

Black Road Access

Black Rd.

Rollins Savanna
Forest Preserve

Trail Length	5.5 miles
Surface	Crushed stone
Location & Setting	Rollins Savanna offers some 5.5 miles of 12 foot-widegravel trail with bridges and boardwalks for biking, hiking and wildlife observation, and .7 miles of 8 foot-wide gravel educational trail loop. It contains scattered groves of majestic oaks, wide-open prairies teeming with wildflowers, native grasses and abundant wetlands. Facilities include drinking water, restrooms, trailside nature education exhibits and observation blinds. The preserve is open from 6:30 a.m. to sunset. The main entrance is off Washington Street across from Atkinson Road, about .2 miles east of Route 83 and 1.4 miles west of Route 45.
Information	Lake County Forest Preserves (847) 367-6640
County	Lake

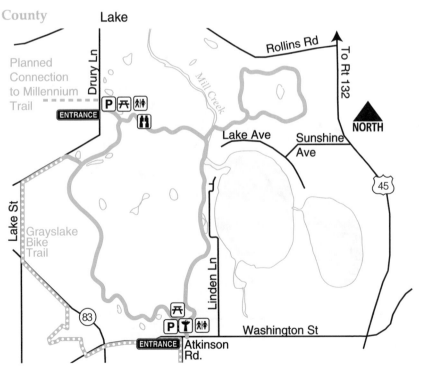

Running Deer Trail

Trail Length	8 miles including alternate trails
Surface	Natural
Location & Setting	The trail is located in Dirksen Park, north of Pekin and Rte 98. It consists of some 450 acres of woodland and meadows. At its highest point it overlooks the Illinois River Valley. The trailhead is on the north side of Route 98, at McNaughton Park Road. Parking is available south of the Archery Range Road on Route 98 and along Pontiac Road in Marquette Heights. The setting is composed of oak-hickory forest and open scrubland. The trail crosses several cobble-bottomed creeks. Winding singletrack, with some challenging climbs and downhills.
Information	Pekin Park District (309) 347-7275
County	Tazewell

Joliet Rd.

Lincoln Rd.

Frontinac Rd.

Pontiac Rd.

NORTH

Dirksen Park

P

T

Rte. 98

McNaughton Park

Salt Creek Bicycle Trail

Trail Length	9.9 miles
Surface	Paved – 6.6 miles; limestone screenings – 3.3 miles
Location & Setting	Located in west central Cook County. Bordered clockwise by the communities of Oakbrook, Westchester, Brookfield, LaGrange Park, LaGrange and Hinsdale. The Salt Creek Trail starts in Bemis Woods South and continues east to Brookfield Woods, directly across from the Brookfield Zoo. As the trail follows Salt Creek, it provides access to various picnic groves and other points of interest. The trail may be accessed from Ogden Avenue, just east of Wolf Road, or from 31st Street between First Avenue and Prairie Avenue.
Information	Forest Preserve District of Cook County (800) 870-3666
County	Cook

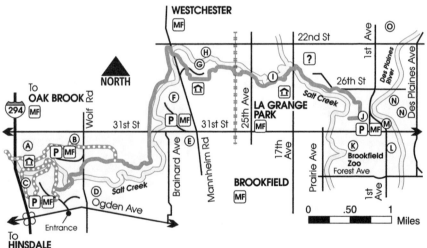

POINTS OF INTEREST

A.	Meadow Lark Golf Course	**I.**	26th Street Woods
B.	Bemis Woods North	**J.**	Brookfield Woods
C.	Bemis Woods South	**K.**	Brookfield Zoo
D.	Salt Creek Nursery	**L.**	Zoo Woods
E.	La Grange Park Woods	**M.**	McCormick Woods
F.	Possum Hollow Woods	**N.**	National Grove-North & South
G.	Brezina Woods	**O.**	Miller Meadows
H.	Westchester Woods		

Skokie Valley Trail

Trail Length	10.0 miles
Surface	Asphalt
Location & Setting	The trail runs both north and south, parallel to Skokie Valley Road, and is built on ComEd right-of-way. It terminates in the south at Lake Cook Road, and in the north at Laurel Avenue. There are overpasses over Deerpath Road, US-41, and at Half Day Road. There is a connection to the Robert McClory Trail at the north end via a tunnel under the Union Pacific tracks.
Information	Lake County Division of Transportation (847) 362-3950
County	Lake

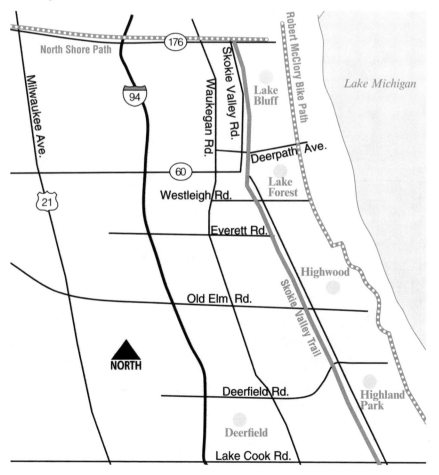

Springbrook Prairie

Trail Length	8.5 miles
Surface	Limestone screening, mowed turf
Location & Setting	Springbrook Prairie is a newly developed 1,849 acre preserve with 8.5 multi-use trail and a 2-mile footpath through wet and dry prairie. Much of this previous farmland is in the process of being restored to native grasses, creating a savanna-like setting. Drinking water, flush toilets, shelters and picnic areas are located throughout the preserve. There are over 6 miles of crushed limestone trail and 2 miles of narrow, mowed trail. Located in Naperville. There are entrances off Plainfield/Naperville Road, between 75th Street and 87th Street.
Information	Forest Preserve District of DuPage County (630) 933-7200
County	DuPage

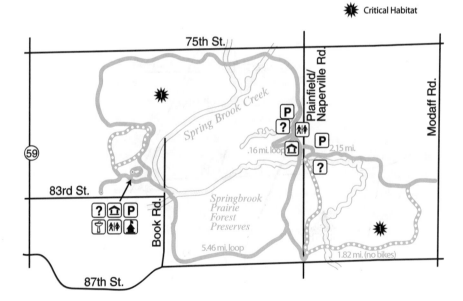

Stone Bridge Trail

Trail Length	5.75 miles
Surface	Screenings
Location & Setting	The trail is built on an abandoned railbed and begins at McCurry Road in Roscoe then proceeds southeast to the Boone county line. The setting is rural with wide open areas and farmland.
Information	Rockford Park District (815) 987-8800
County	Winnebago

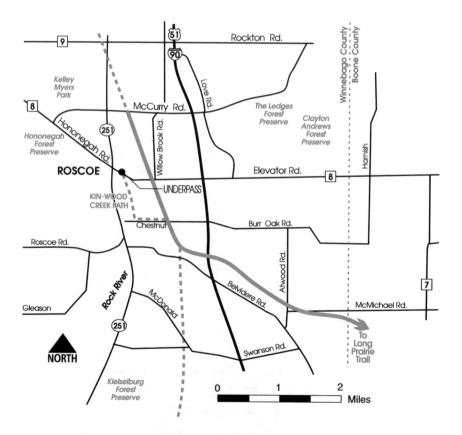

The Stone Bridge Trail joins the Long Prairie Trail at the Boone County line.

Sugar Creek Preserve
Wauponsee Glacial Trail

Trail Length	26 miles
Surface	Asphalt, crushed limestone
Location & Setting	The Wauponsee Glacial Trail, located in the Sugar Creek Preserve, follows the abandoned rail lines from Joliet to Kankakee and is named after an ancient glacial lake. A 15-mile segment from Joliet to Symerton is now complete. The trail north of Laraway Road is asphalt, and south of Laraway Road is limestone screenings. There is access to the trail and parking at the Sugar Creek Administration Center in Joliet, Manhattan Road in Manhattan, or Commercial Drive in Symerton. The Sugar Creek Preserve is located at 17540 West Laraway Road, about ¾ miles west of Route 52. Preserve hours are 8 am to 8 pm.
Information	Forest Preserve District of Will County (815) 727-8700
County	Will

Sun Lake Forest Preserve

Trail Length	3.3 miles
Surface	Crushed gravel
Location & Setting	Sun Lake, with 580-acres, features a landscape of oak woodlands and wetlands, and includes Sun Lake. This lake provides an example of an Illinois glacial lake. Due to the unstable shoreline, access to the lake itself is not permitted. The trail was designed for nature and wildlife observation. Three trail spurs connect to the North Shore on Deep Lake Subdivision, the Lake Villa Baseball Park, and Longwood Centre Park.
Information	Lake County Forest Preserves (847) 367-6640
County	Lake

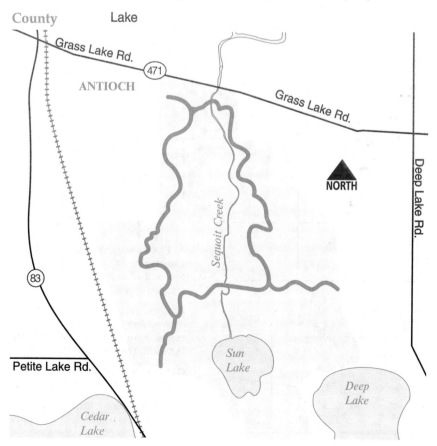

Thorn Creek Forest Preserve

Trail Length & Surface	Red, Brown, Purple & Black Loop Trails – 14.2 miles paved, Yellow & Black Trails – 4.9 miles screenings
Location & Setting	The Thorn Creek Bicycle Trail is located in far south Cook County. One section consists of trail through the Sauk Trail lake area and another winds through Lansing Woods and North Creek Meadow. A future extension will link these sections. Access the western section along Ashland Avenue, and the eastern section from either Glenwood-Lansing Road or 183rd Street east of Torrence Avenue. It is bounded clockwise by the communities of South Holland, Lansing, Chicago Heights, South Chicago Heights, Park Forest, Olympia Fields, Glenwood and Thornton.
Information	Forest Preserve District of Cook County (800) 870-3666
County	Cook

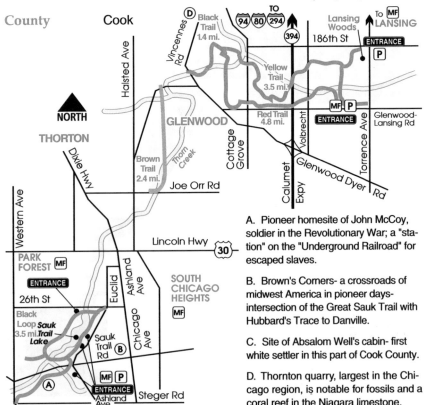

A. Pioneer homesite of John McCoy, soldier in the Revolutionary War; a "station" on the "Underground Railroad" for escaped slaves.

B. Brown's Corners- a crossroads of midwest America in pioneer days- intersection of the Great Sauk Trail with Hubbard's Trace to Danville.

C. Site of Absalom Well's cabin- first white settler in this part of Cook County.

D. Thornton quarry, largest in the Chicago region, is notable for fossils and a coral reef in the Niagara limestone.

Tinley Creek Forest Preserve

Trail Length   24.8 miles

Surface   Paved & a 1.2-mile unpaved spur

Location & Setting   The Tinley Creek Bicycle Trail is located in southwestern Cook County. The trail passes through gently rolling country, forests, prairies and alongside wetlands. It is bordered (clockwise) by the communities of Palos Heights, Crestwood, Oak Forest, Country Club Hills, Flossmoor, Tinley Park and Orland Park.

Information   Forest Preserve District of Cook County (800) 870-3666

County   Cook

Pause along 159th Street, just east of Oak Park Avenue, for an unusual view of the Chicago skyline, approximately 20 miles to the northeast.

There are accesses and parking along Central Avenue between 159th Street and 175th Street in the northern section. Access and parking to the southern loop is available off both Vollmer and Flossmoor Roads. A future extension will link these two sections.

A. Arrowhead Lake Access Area
B. Elizabeth A. Conkey Forest
C. Turtlehead Lake Access Area
D. Rubio Woods
E. The George W. Dunne National Golf Course
F. Yankee Woods
G. Midlothian Reservoir (Twin Lakes)
H. Midlothian Meadows
I. St. Mihiel West
J. Vollmer Road Picnic

Tunnel Hill State Trail

Trail Length	45 miles
Surface	Crushed stone
Location & Setting	The Tunnel Hill Trail stretches from Harrisburg to Kamak, and then continues on a 2.5 mile spur from Kamak to Cache River State Natural Area. The 9 mile section between Tunnel Hill and Vienna crosses the American Discovery Trail and the Trail of Tears. A ¼ mile south of Tunnel Hill is a 543-feet long tunnel, the only one on the trail. The route includes 23 picturesque trestles, ranging in length from 34 to 450 feet, with the Breeden Trestle being the highest at 80 feet. Drinking water, privy toilets and parking can be found at access areas.
Information	Tunnel Hill State Trail (618)658-2168
	Shawnee National Forest Forest Supervisor (800) MY WOODS
Counties	Saline, Williamson and Johnson

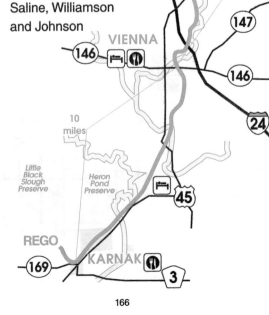

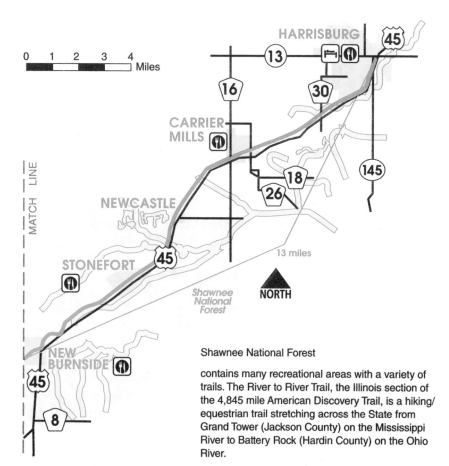

Scale: 0 1 2 3 4 Miles

HARRISBURG

(45)

(13)

(16)

(30)

CARRIER MILLS

(145)

(18)

(26)

MATCH LINE

NEWCASTLE

13 miles

(45)

▲ NORTH

STONEFORT

Shawnee National Forest

NEW BURNSIDE

(45)

(8)

Shawnee National Forest

contains many recreational areas with a variety of trails. The River to River Trail, the Illinois section of the 4,845 mile American Discovery Trail, is a hiking/ equestrian trail stretching across the State from Grand Tower (Jackson County) on the Mississippi River to Battery Rock (Hardin County) on the Ohio River.

Points of Interest:

Garden of the Gods Located southeast of Harrisburg in Saline County, Garden of the Gods attracts thousands of visitors each year with its incredible rock formations, such as Camel Rock, Devil's Needle, Noah's Ark, Anvil Rock, and Tower of Babel. Eight miles of hiking trails bring visitors to the rock formations. The rocks can be climbed as well as viewed. The best time of year is the fall when the Shawnee Hills form a fiery backdrop to the formations. For more information call 618/287-2001.

Vadalabene Bike Trail

Trail Length	19 miles
Surface	Paved
Location & Setting	This path follows Route 100 between Alton, Grafton, and to Pere Marquette State Park. The bikeway is bordered by towering limestone cliffs and the Mississippi River, and is a recreational destination for bicycle enthusiasts.
Information	Illinois Dept. of Transportation (217) 782-7820
	Southern Illinois Tourism Council Box 286 Belleville, IL 62222
Counties	Madison, Jersey

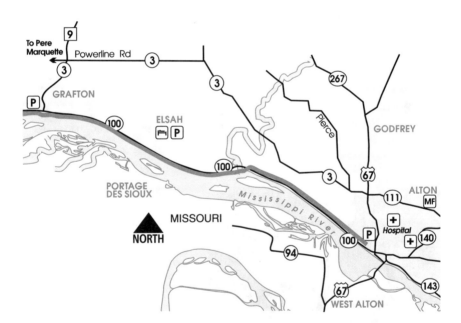

The northern section follows the wide paved shoulders of the McAdams Parkway to Grafton. The southern section is a separate paved path built on an abandoned railroad line at the base of the bluffs. There are parking areas along and at each end of the bikeway. Pause to visit the historic town of Grafton and Elsah with their antique shops.

Vernon Hills Trails

Trail Length	7.0 miles
Surface	Paved
Location & Setting	Vernon Hills is located in central Lake County.

Century Park – Route 60 west ¾ miles of Route 21 to Lakeview Parkway. Turn north for ½ mile to the park.

Deerpath – Route 60 past Lakeview Parkway to Deerpath Drive. Turn south and proceed to Cherokee Road. Turn east (left) to Deerpath Park.

Information	Vernon Hills Park District	(847) 996-6800
County	Lake	

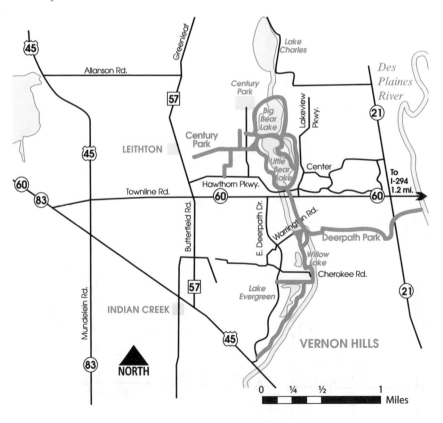

Open field and some woods. Exercise stations surround the lake in Century Park. The path runs through Deerpath Park playgrounds, tennis courts and a small lake.

Veteran Acres Park

Trail Length	3.0 miles
Surface	Natural
Location & Setting	Located on the north side of Crystal Lake. Access from Terra Cotta Road from the south or Walkup Road from the west. Rolling hills, woods, prairie, recreational areas. Facilities include a Nature Center, restrooms, picnic shelters, and playground.
Information	Crystal Lake Park District (815) 459-0680
County	McHenry

Sterne's Woods can be accessed from Veteran Acres and has about two miles of dirt road open to hiking.

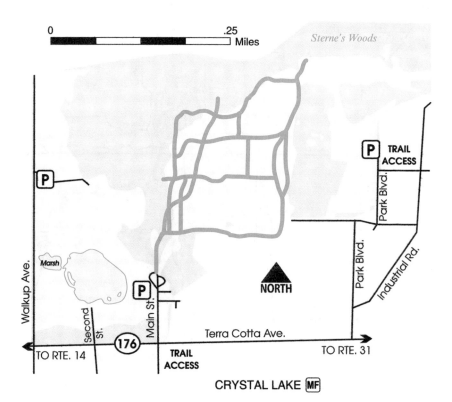

Virgil L. Gilman Nature Trail

Trail Length	10.5 miles
Surface	Paved
Location & Setting	The trail stretches west uninterrupted past farmlands straddling the Kane and Kendall County border. The Virgil Gilman Trail passes rural, urban and suburban areas.
Information	Fox River Park District (630) 897-0516
County	Kane

Aurora is the largest community in Kane County. It was the first midwest community to electrically illuminate its streets.

Services are available at Parker Avenue, Elmwood Drive, Orchard Road, Blackberry Village and Bliss Woods.

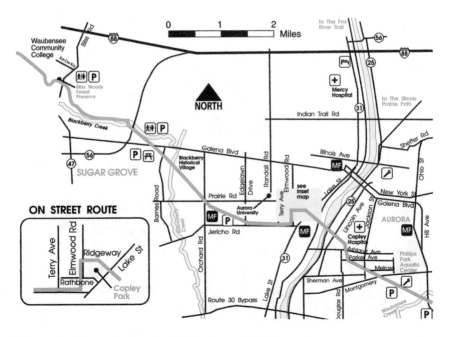

The rural landscape gives way to city life when entering Aurora.

Waterfall Glen Forest Preserve

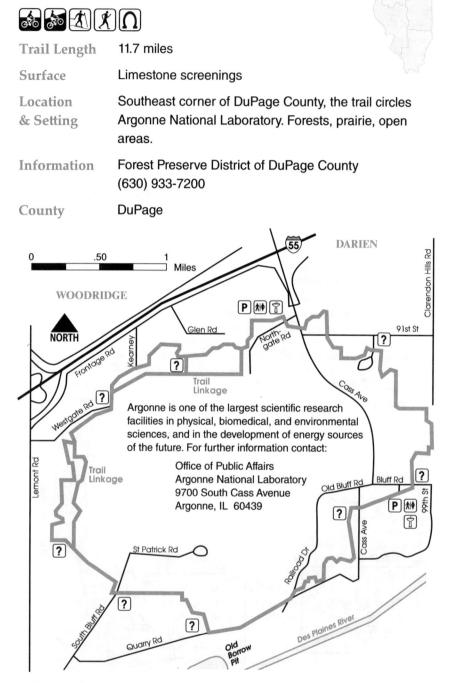

Trail Length	11.7 miles
Surface	Limestone screenings
Location & Setting	Southeast corner of DuPage County, the trail circles Argonne National Laboratory. Forests, prairie, open areas.
Information	Forest Preserve District of DuPage County (630) 933-7200
County	DuPage

Argonne is one of the largest scientific research facilities in physical, biomedical, and environmental sciences, and in the development of energy sources of the future. For further information contact:

Office of Public Affairs
Argonne National Laboratory
9700 South Cass Avenue
Argonne, IL 60439

WATERFALL GLEN PRESERVE Waterfall Glen provides some of the best bicycling, cross country skiing and hiking in DuPage County. The main trail is 8 feet wide. In addition, there are many mowed grass trails and footpaths through the preserve.

West DuPage Woods Forest Preserve

Trail Length	3.7 miles
Surface	Natural, groomed
Location & Setting	This 462-acre preserve is located on Route 59, about a half mile north of Roosevelt Road. There is a second entrance on Gary's Mill Road, between Roosevelt and Winfield roads. The mowed paths take you through upland woods, open meadow, and riparian habitats. Facilities include picnic areas a water pump, toilet, and horse trailer parking.
Information	Forest Preserve District of DuPage County (630) 933-7200
County	DuPage

High Lake

Forest Ave.

White Pine Trail
0.2 miles

P

?

W. Branch DuPage River

Red Oak Trail
1.1 miles

59

Neltnor Ave.

Goldenrod Trail
0.7 miles

Hickory Trail
1.1 miles

Aster Trail
0.1 miles

NORTH

38

Willow Trail
0.7 miles

P

Roosevelt Rd.

Gary's Mill Rd.

- - - - **Connector**

Wright Woods Forest Preserve
Half Day Forest Preserve

Trail Length   4 miles

Surface   Crushed gravel

Location & Setting   Located north of Routes 45/22 (Old Half Day Road), the 502-acre Wright Woods connects to the Des Plaines River Trail and is linked to the 201-acre Half Day Preserve by a footbridge spanning the river. Wright Woods supports large stands of rich oak and maple woodland. Facilities at Half Day include 3 picnic shelters, drinking water, comfort stations, grills, electricity, horseshoe pits, and grass fields.

Information   Lake County Forest Preserves   (847) 367-6640

County   Lake

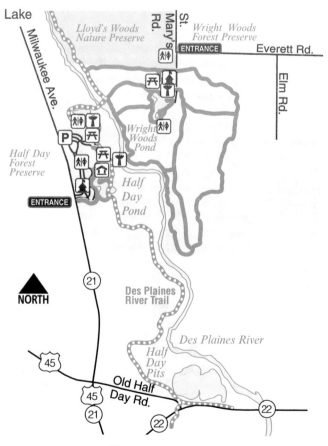

Zion Bicycle Path

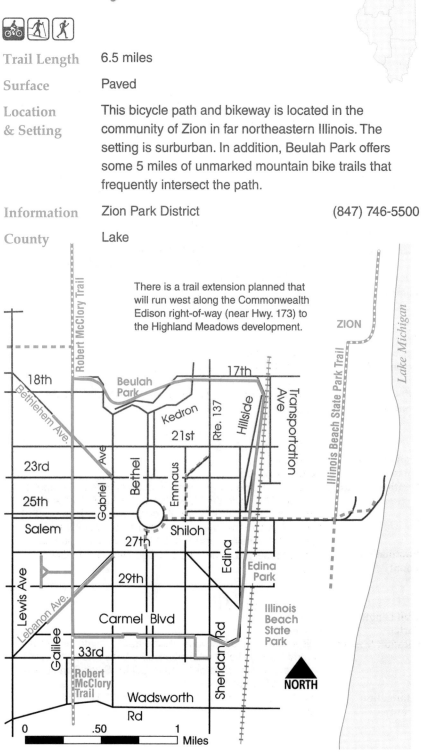

Trail Length	6.5 miles
Surface	Paved
Location & Setting	This bicycle path and bikeway is located in the community of Zion in far northeastern Illinois. The setting is surburban. In addition, Beulah Park offers some 5 miles of unmarked mountain bike trails that frequently intersect the path.
Information	Zion Park District (847) 746-5500
County	Lake

There is a trail extension planned that will run west along the Commonwealth Edison right-of-way (near Hwy. 173) to the Highland Meadows development.

ZION

Lake Michigan

Robert McClory Trail

Illinois Beach State Park Trail

18th

Bethlehem Ave.

Beulah Park

17th

Kedron

21st

Rte. 137

Hillside

Transportation Ave

23rd

Gabriel Ave

Bethel

Emmaus

25th

Salem

27th

Shiloh

Edina

Edina Park

Lewis Ave

Lebanon Ave.

29th

Galilee

Carmel Blvd

Sheridan Rd

Illinois Beach State Park

33rd

Robert McClory Trail

Wadsworth Rd

NORTH

0	.50	1

Miles

Additional Trails

Anderson Memorial Path 🚴 🏃 🚶

Trail Length	3 miles
Location & Setting	Paved
	This path follows Kent Creek between Talcott-Page and Lockwood parks in Rockford. In addition to these two parks, the path can be accessed at Searls Park at Kilburn and Central Avenue, or the Northwest Community Center at 1325 N Johnston Avenue. Searls Park also features a beautiful natural prairie.
Information	Rockford Park District (815) 987-8800
County	Winnebago

Bartlett's Trails & Bikeways 🚴 🏃

Trail Length	15 miles
Location & Setting	Bartlett. There is a trailhead on Route 50 between Routes 59 and 43 and at the intersection of Routes 59 and 6.
Information	Bartlett Park District (630) 540-4800
County	Cook

Belleville's Trails & Bikeways 🚴 🏃

Trail Length	6 miles
Surface	Crushed stone
Location & Setting	East Belleville. Trailheads at the junction of Routes 44 and 89 and the junction of Routes 158 and 159.
Information	Belleville Chamber of Commerce (618) 233-2015
County	St. Clair

Burnham Greenway 🚴 🏃 🛼

Trail Length	4.7 miles
Surface	Paved, unpaved
Location & Setting	Chicago. The path runs north and south from Indianapolis Blvd. & 104th St. to Wolf Lake Rd. & Avenue O for 2.4 miles. It then continues from State St. to the Calumet River for 2.3 miles. The Greenway surface is currently a combination of paved and unpaved, and is open from sunrise to sunset.
Information	Forest Preserve District of Cook County(800) 870-3666
County	Cook

Butler Lake Bike Path 🚴 🏃

Trail Length	4 miles
Surface	Asphalt
Location & Setting	This 4-mile, 4 to 6 foot wide, paved trail is located in north central Libertyville. It encircles Butler Lake and continues north, across Winchester Road to Gilbert Stiles Park, then northwest to Paul Neal Park.
Information	Libertyville Parks Dept. (847) 918-7275
County	Lake

Calumet-Sag Trail 🚴 🚶

Trail Length	26 miles planned, 1mile complete
Surface	Asphalt
Location & Setting	This planned trail project in the near-south suburbs of the Chicago area will stretch from the Burnham Greenway west to the confluence of the Calumet-Sag Channel, the I&M Canal and the Sanitary and Ship Canal. It involves the coalition of 14 communities. The only portion currently complete at the time of this printing is between Harlem Avenue and the Lake Katherine Nature Preserve.
Information	National Park Service (312) 427-3325
County	Cook

Chain Of Lakes Bike Path 🚴 🚶 ⛸

Trail Length	3 miles
Surface	Asphalt
Location & Setting	This trail parallels the south side of Rollins Rd in Fox Lake. It runs from Sayton Rd eastward to where it connects to the Grant Woods Forest Preserve Trail, .8 miles east of Wilson Rd. There is an underpass at Route 59, but it's a road crossing at Wilson Rd. From the east take Belvidere Rd (Route 120) to Cedar Lake Rd, then north to Rollins Rd.
Information	Lake County Dept. of Transportation (847) 382-3750
County	Lake

Dekalb/Sycamore Trail 🚴 🚶 ⛷

Trail Length	6 miles
Surface	Paved
Location & Setting	The DeKalb/Sycamore Trail is 6 miles long, paved, and links the DeKalb Park District Trail from Lions Park on DeKalb's south side to Sycamore and the Great Western Trail.
Information	County Forest Preserve (815) 527-4005
County	DeKalb

El Paso Trail 🚴 🚶

Trail Length	2.7 miles
Surface	Crushed stone
Location & Setting	Town of El Paso
Information	City Hall, 52 North Elm, El Paso, IL 61738 (309) 527-4005
County	Woodford

Gaylord Donnelley Canal Trail 🚴 🚶 ⛸ ⛷

Trail Length	5 miles
Surface	Paved
Location & Setting	A 5 mile paved trail running between Joliet and Lockport, forming part of the I&M Canal corridor.
Information	Will County Forest Preserve (815) 727-8700
County	Will

Additional Trails (continued)

Green Diamond Trail 🚲🚶🛼⛷

Trail Length	5.5 miles
Surface	Asphalt
Location & Setting	A flat, easy trail located in Montgomery County, and built on abandoned Illinois Central railroad corridor. There is trail access at the south end of Cleveland Street in Farmersville and at the Historic Depot Park on Main Street in Waggoner.
Information	Montgomery County Coordinator 217-532-9577
County	Montgomery

HUM Trail 🚲🚶🛷⛷

Trail Length	3.5 miles
Surface	Crushed limestone
Location & Setting	The Huntley-Union–Marengo Trail currently runs from East Street. in Marengo to Vine Street in Union, and is open from sunrise to sunset. There is parking off Prospect Street in Marengo. Future plans include an extension of the trail to 17 miles, running from the Boone County line to Huntley.
Information	McHenry County Conservation District(815) 338-6223
County	McHenry

Interurban Trail 🚲🚶🛼

Trail Length	7 miles
Surface	Asphalt
Location & Setting	The Interurban Trail was built on abandoned Interurban Railroad Right-of-Way in Springfield. It begins at the corner of Wabash Avenue and MacArthur Blvd., and proceeds in a southerly direction to Woodside Road.
Information	Springfield Park District (217) 544-1751
County	Sangamon

John Humphrey Trail 🚲🚶🛼⛷

Trail Length	3 miles
Surface	Paved
Location & Setting	The John Humphrey Trail is located in Orland Park, and connects the Village Center and Metra station. It's 3 miles long and surfaced. The setting is urban, with woods and nearby wetlands.
Information	Village of Orland Park (708) 403-6100
County	Cook

Lyons Woods Forest Preserve 🚲🚶⛷

Trail Length	3 miles
Surface	Crushed gravel
Location & Setting	This preserve offers a diverse mix or prairie, savanna, pine grove, forest and fen. Lyons Woods is near Waukegan and Beach Park. From downtown Waukegan, take Sheridan Rd. north to Blanchard Rd. and turn left for a short distance to the entrance. Facilities include drinking water and restrooms. The trail ties into the North Shore Path, which in turn connects to other community trails.
Information	Lake County Forest Preserve (847) 367-6640
County	Lake

Major Taylor Trail 🚴 🚶

Trail Length	6.5 miles
Surface	Paved
Location & Setting	Located on Chicago's South Side, the 6.5 mile trail opened in June, 2007. It runs between the Dan Ryan Woods near 80th Place and Whistler Woods on the south bank of the Little Calumet River in Riverdale. The trail is named after the African-American bicycle racing legend of the 1890's.
Information	Chicago Park District (312) 742-7929
County	Cook

Mallard Lake Forest Preserve 🚴 🚶 🏕 🎿

Trail Length	2.5 miles
Surface	Groomed
Location & Setting	The Mallard Lake Forest Preserve winds through and over a mixture of habitats including open water, grassy fields and scattered woodlands. The trail can be accessed from the parking area and will lead you through the preserve's picnic area and around and across Mallard Lake over two bridges. The terrain is relatively level and trail surface is limestone screenings and mowed turf. Located in Bloomingdale off the intersection of Lawrence Ave. and Cloverdale Rd.
Information	Forest Preserve District of DuPage County (630) 933-7200
County	DuPage

Meecham Grove Forest Preserve 🚴 🚶 🎿

Trail Length	2.6 miles
Surface	Crushed limestone
Location & Setting	The trail system in this 251-acre preserve crosses diverse habitats, such as great egrets, blue herons, and beaver. You can access the trail from a parking lot located on Circle Ave. From the loop circling Maple Lake the trail heads west and crosses Bloomingdale/Roselle Rd. as a pedestrian bridge.
Information	Forest Preserve District of DuPage County (630) 933-7200
County	DuPage

Midewin National Tallgrass Prairie 🚴 🚶 🏕

Trail Length	17 plus miles
Surface	Old park roads
Location & Setting	Midewin has 7,200 acres open to the public, and is located in northeastern IL near the town of Wilmington. The trails are currently temporary and follow designated routes on old roads of varying quality. There is a Welcome Center with water and flush toilets. Hours are an hour before sunrise until an hour after sunset.
Information	Midewin National Tallgrass Prairie (815)423-6370
County	Will

Newton Lake Fish & Wildlife Area 🚴 🚶 🏕 🎿

Trail Length	4.5 miles
Surface	Natural
Location & Setting	4.5 mile biking trail located SW of Newton in southern IL. From Newton; S on 1100E to 700N, W to 300N, S to 500N, then E to the entrance. There are 4.5 miles of mountain biking trail, plus 22 miles of hiking, cross-country skiing and equestrian use along the picturesque shoreline of the lake. The trail system begins at the North Access parking lot.
Information	Newton Lake Fish & Wildlife Area (618) 783-3478
County	Jasper

Additional Trails (continued)

Nippersink Forest Preserve 🚲 🚶 ⛷

Trail Length	2.5 miles
Surface	Crushed limestone
Location & Setting	The 309-acre preserve is located in west central Lake County near Round Lake. The entrance is off Rte. 120 just west of Cedar Lake Rd. Amenities include a boardwalk, scenic overlook, drinking fountains, and comfort station. The setting consists of two scenic lakes, woodlands, wetlands and marshes.
Information	Lake County Forest Preserves (847) 367-6640
County	Lake

Pioneer Parkway 🚲 🚶 ⛷

Trail Length	2.5 miles
Surface	Crushed stone
Location & Setting	From Peoria to Alta
Information	Peoria Park District (309) 682-1200
County	Peoria

Van Patten Woods 🚲 🚶 ⛷

Trail Length	4 miles
Surface	Crushed stone
Location & Setting	This 901-acre Preserve surrounds the 94-acre Sterling Lake, which is the center of activity. Each of the lake's two basins is encircled by a 1-mile trail. On the Preserve's eastern half are a 2-mile multi-use loop trail and a 1-mile loop limited to hikers and cross-country skiers. Facilities include a boat and canoe launch, picnic areas, youth campground, and a model airplane field.
Information	Lake County Forest Preserves (847) 367-6640
County	Lake

Wabash Trail 🚲 🚶 🛼

Trail Length	3 miles
Surface	Paved
Location & Setting	Located on Springfield's southeast side, it follows an old railroad right-of-way. The trail begins near the intersection of MacArthur Blvd. and Wabash Avenue, and continues west to Park Avenue, and then Chatham Road, finally terminating at Robbins Road. Parking is available at Park Avenue, and also at Vredenburgh and Westchester parks. The setting is a combination of residential, commercial and some industrial.
Information	Springfield Visitors Bureau 800-545-7300
County	Sangamon

Waubonsie Trail 🚲 🚶 🛼 ⛷

Trail Length	2.5 miles
Surface	Paved
Location & Setting	Town of Oswego, S of Aurora. Surface is asphalt, setting urban parkland.
Information	Oswego Park District (630) 554-1010
County	Kendall

Find me a place, safe and serene,

Away from the terror I see on the screen.

A place where my soul can find some peace,

Away from the stress and the pressures released.

A corridor of green not far from my home

For fresh air and exercise, quiet will roam.

Summer has smells that tickle my nose

And fall has the leaves that crunch under my toes.

Beware, comes a person we pass in a while

with a wave and hello and a wide friendly smile.

Recreation trails are the place to be,

To find that safe haven of peace and serenity.

By Beverly Moore
Illinois Trails Conservancy

Selected Illinois State Parks

North West Region

North West Region Park Name	Acreage	Concession	Drinking Water	Rest rooms	Bike Trails	Boat Rentals	Canoe Access	Canoe Rental	Hiking	Camping
		FACILITIES					ACTIVITIES			
Argyle Lake State Park	1700	●	●	♿		●	●		●	AB/CDY
Big River State Forest	3027		♿	♿			●		●	CD
Castle Rock State Park	1995		●	●			●		●	Canoe
Delabar State Park	89		●	●			●		●	B/ECD
Hennepin Canal Parkway State Park	5773		♿	♿	●		●		♿	CDY
Ilini State Park	510	●	●	♿			●		●	B/ECY
Johnson-Sauk Trail State Park	1361	●	♿	♿		●	●		●	B/E♿DY
Jubilee College State Park	3500		♿	♿					●	AB/SC♿
Lake Le-Aqua-Na State Park	715	●	●	♿		●	●		♿	AB/SCY
Lowden State Park	2234	●	♿	♿			●		●	AB/SD
Mississippi Palisades State Park	2505	●	●	♿			●		●	AB/SDY A♿B/
Rock Cut State Park	3092	●	♿	♿	●	●	●		●	SCY
Rock Island Trail State Park	392		♿	♿	●				●	D
Starved Rock State Park	2630	♿	♿	♿			●		●	A♿YL
White Pines Forest State Park	385	♿	●	♿					●	CY

CLASS **A** SITES   Showers, electricity & vehicular access *(fee)*

CLASS **B/E** SITES   Electricity & vehicular access *(fee)*

CLASS **B/S** SITES   Showers & vehicular access *(fee)*

CLASS **C** SITES   Vehicular access *(fee)*

CLASS **D** SITES   Tent camping/primitive sites (walk in/backpack) no vehicular access *(fee)*

CLASS **Y** SITES   Youth Groups only

♿   Accessible to visitors with disabilities

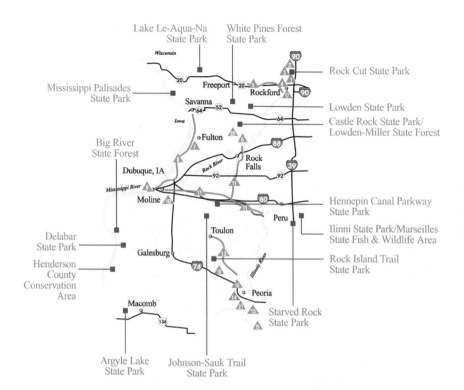

Lake Le-Aqua-Na State Park; White Pines Forest State Park; Mississippi Palisades State Park; Rock Cut State Park; Lowden State Park; Castle Rock State Park/Lowden-Miller State Forest; Big River State Forest; Dubuque, IA; Hennepin Canal Parkway State Park; Ilinni State Park/Marseilles State Fish & Wildlife Area; Delabar State Park; Rock Island Trail State Park; Henderson County Conservation Area; Starved Rock State Park; Argyle Lake State Park; Johnson-Sauk Trail State Park

North East Region

North East Region Park Name	Acreage	FACILITIES				ACTIVITIES				
		Concession	Drinking Water	Rest rooms	Bike Trails	Boat Rentals	Canoe Access	Canoe Rental	Hiking	Camping
Chain O'Lakes State Park	6063	●	&	&	●	●	●	●		AB/SY
Channahon State Park	25		●	●	●		●		●	DY
Des Plaines Conservation Area	5012	●	●	&			●		●	C
Gebhard Woods State Park	30		&	●			●		●	DY
Goose Lake Prairie State Nat'l. Area	2468		●	&					●	
I & M Canal State Trail	2802		●	●	●		●		●	D
Illinois Beach State Park	4160	&	&	&	●		●		&	A&YL
Kankakee River State Park	3932	&	&	&	●		●	●	●	A&B/ECDY
Moraine Hills State Park	1763	●	&	●	●	●			●	
Silver Springs State Park	1314	●	●	&			●	●	●	DY

CLASS **A** SITES   Showers, electricity & vehicular access *(fee)*

CLASS **B/E** SITES   Electricity & vehicular access *(fee)*

CLASS **B/S** SITES   Showers & vehicular access *(fee)*

CLASS **C** SITES   Vehicular access *(fee)*

CLASS **D** SITES   Tent camping/primitive sites (walk in/backpack) no vehicular access *(fee)*

CLASS **Y** SITES   Youth Groups only

        & Accessible to visitors with disabilities

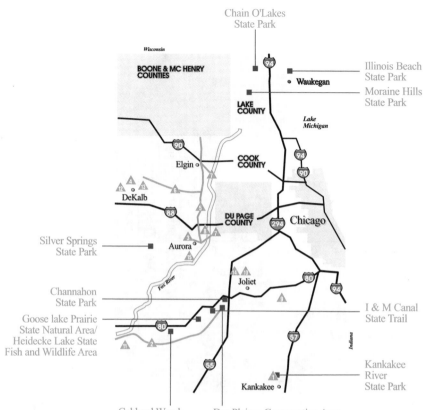

Chain O'Lakes State Park

Wisconsin

BOONE & MC HENRY COUNTIES

Waukegan

Illinois Beach State Park

Moraine Hills State Park

LAKE COUNTY

Lake Michigan

Elgin

COOK COUNTY

DeKalb

DU PAGE COUNTY

Chicago

Silver Springs State Park

Aurora

Fox River

Channahon State Park

Joliet

Goose lake Prairie State Natural Area/ Heidecke Lake State Fish and Wildlife Area

I & M Canal State Trail

Indiana

Kankakee River State Park

Kankakee

Gebhard Woods State Park/ William G. Stratton State Park

Des Plaines Conservation Area

East Central Region

East Central Region Park Name	Acreage	FACILITIES			ACTIVITIES					
		Concession	Drinking Water	Rest rooms	Bike Trails	Boat Rentals	Canoe Access	Canoe Rental	Hiking	Camping
Clinton Lake State Recreation Area	9915		♿	♿		•			•	B/SY
Eagle Creek State Recreation Area	1463		•	♿					•	B/ECY
Fox Ridge State Park	1517		•	♿					•	B/SY
Hidden Springs State Forest	1121		•	♿					•	CY
Kickapoo State Park	2844	•	•	♿	•	•	•	•	•	AB/SCDYR
Lincoln Trail State Park	1022	♿	•	♿		•	•	•	•	A♿DY
Moraine View State Park	1688	♿	♿	♿		•	•		♿	B/ED
Walnut Point State Fish & Wildlife Area	592	•	•	♿		•	•		•	B/EDY
Weldon Springs State Park	370	•	•	♿		•	•		•	B/EDY
Wolf Creek State Park	1967		•	♿					•	RACDY

CLASS **A** SITES   Showers, electricity & vehicular access *(fee)*

CLASS **B/E** SITES   Electricity & vehicular access *(fee)*

CLASS **B/S** SITES   Showers & vehicular access *(fee)*

CLASS **C** SITES   Vehicular access *(fee)*

CLASS **D** SITES   Tent camping/primitive sites (walk in/backpack) no vehicular access *(fee)*

CLASS **Y** SITES   Youth Groups only

♿   Accessible to visitors with disabilities

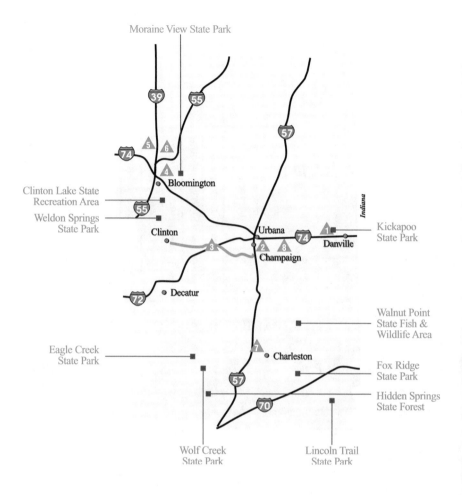

West Central Region

West Central Region Park Name	Acreage	Concession	Drinking Water	Rest rooms	Bike Trails	Boat Rentals	Canoe Access	Canoe Rental	Hiking	Camping
		FACILITIES				ACTIVITIES				
Beaver Dam State Park	744	●	●	♿		●	●		●	AB/SY
Horseshoe Lake State Park	2854		●	♿			●		●	C♿
Nauvoo State Park	148		♿	♿			●		●	B/ECY
Pere Marquette State Park	7901	●	●	♿	●				●	A♿B/SYL
Randolph County State F & W Area	1021	●	●	♿		●	●		●	C♿DY
Sand Ridge State Forest	7112		●	●					●	CDY
Sangchris Lake State Park	3576	●		♿			●			B/ECDY
Siloam Springs State Park	3323	♿	♿	♿		●	●		●	A♿B/SD
Washington Cnty Conservation Area	1440	♿	♿	♿		●	●		●	A♿CY
Weinberg-King State Park	772		●	♿					●	C♿Y

CLASS **A** SITES   Showers, electricity & vehicular access *(fee)*

CLASS **B/E** SITES   Electricity & vehicular access *(fee)*

CLASS **B/S** SITES   Showers & vehicular access *(fee)*

CLASS **C** SITES   Vehicular access *(fee)*

CLASS **D** SITES   Tent camping/primitive sites (walk in/backpack) no vehicular access *(fee)*

CLASS **Y** SITES   Youth Groups only

♿   Accessible to visitors with disabilities

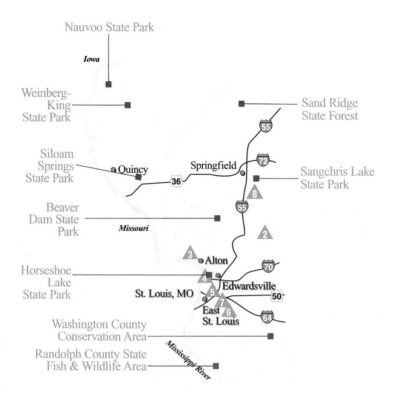

Nauvoo State Park

Iowa

Weinberg-
King
State Park

Sand Ridge
State Forest

Siloam
Springs
State Park
○ Quincy

Springfield

Sangchris Lake
State Park

Beaver
Dam State
Park

Missouri

Horseshoe
Lake
State Park

Alton

St. Louis, MO

Edwardsville

East
St. Louis

Washington County
Conservation Area

Randolph County State
Fish & Wildlife Area

Mississippi River

South Region

South Region Park Name	FACILITIES				ACTIVITIES					
	Acreage	Concession	Drinking Water	Rest rooms	Bike Trails	Boat Rentals	Canoe Access	Canoe Rental	Hiking	Camping
Cave-in-Rock State Park	204	●	●	♿			●		●	B/ECDY
Dixon Springs State Park	787	♿	♿	♿				●	●	B/ED&Y
Ferne Clyffe State Park	1125		♿	♿					●	ADY
Fort Massac State Park	1499		♿	♿			●		●	A&B/S
Giant City State Park	3694	♿	♿	♿			●	●	♿	A&DYL
Hamilton County Conservation Area	1683	●	●	●		●	●		●	B/EDY
Horseshoe Lake Conservation Area	9550		♿	♿			●			A&B/EC
Lake Murphysboro State Park	1024	♿	●	♿		●	●		●	A/ECY
Pyramid State Park	2528		●	●			●		●	CD
Ramsey Lake State Park	1881	●	●	♿		●	●		●	AB,ECDY
Red Hills State Park	948	●	●	♿		●	●		●	A&DY
Sam Dale Lake Conservation Area	1301	●	♿	♿		●	●		●	B/ED&Y
Sam Parr State Park	1133		●	●					●	CDY
Trail of Tears State Forest	4993		●	●					●	DCY
Wayne Fitzgerrell State Park	3300	●	●	●		●		●	●	AD

CLASS **A** SITES   Showers, electricity & vehicular access *(fee)*

CLASS **B/E** SITES   Electricity & vehicular access *(fee)*

CLASS **B/S** SITES   Showers & vehicular access *(fee)*

CLASS **C** SITES   Vehicular access *(fee)*

CLASS **D** SITES   Tent camping/primitive sites (walk in/backpack) no vehicular access *(fee)*

CLASS **Y** SITES   Youth Groups only

♿   Accessible to visitors with disabilities

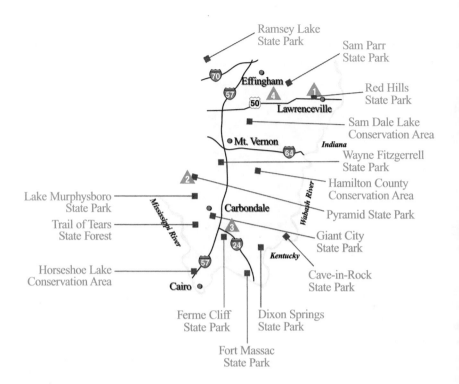

Trail Index

Index (continued)

City to Trail Index

POPULATION CODE

① under 1,000 ② 1,000-4,999 ③ 5,000-9,999 ④ 10,000-49,999 ⑤ 50,000 and over

City to Trail Index (continued)

① under 1,000 ② 1,000-4,999 ③ 5,000-9,999 ④ 10,000-49,999 ⑤ 50,000 and over

City Name	Pop. Code	Trail Name	Page No.
Poplar Grove	①	Long Prairie Trail	110
Port Byron	②	Great River Trail	74
Princeton	③	Hennepin Canal Parkway	80
Princeville	②	Rock Island State Trail	150
Richmond	②	Hebron Trail	178
Richmond	②	Prairie Trail	138
Ringwood	②	Prairie Trail	138
Rochester	②	Lost Bridge Trail	109
Rock Falls	③	Hennepin Canal Parkway	80
Rock Island	④	Great River Trail	74
Rockford	⑤	Anderson Memorial Path	176
Rockford	⑤	Hononegah Recreation Path	85
Rockford	⑤	Pecatonica Prairie Path	132
Rockford	⑤	Rock Cut State Park	148
Rockford	⑤	Rock River & Sportscore Path	154
Rockton	②	Hononegah Recreation Path	85
Roscoe	②	Hononegah Recreation Path	85
Roscoe	②	Stone Bridge Trail	161
Round Lake	④	Nippersink Forest Preserve	180
Round Lk Hgts	②	Grant Woods FP	72
Roxana	②	Watershed Trail	32
Savanna	②	Great River Trail	74
Schaumburg	⑤	Busse Woods FP Trail	41
Schiller Park	④	Des Plaines Trail System - South	60
Seneca	②	I & M Canal State Trail	86
Sheffield	①	Hennepin Canal Parkway	80
South Barrington	②	Poplar Creek Trail	135
South Holland	④	Thorn Creek Bicycle Trail	164
Springfield	⑤	Interurban Trail	178
Springfield	⑤	Lost Bridge Trail	109
Springfield	⑤	Wabash Trail	180
St. Charles	④	Fox River Trail	66
St. Charles	④	Great Western Trail	73
St. Charles	④	Illinois Prairie Path	90
Stonefort	①	Tunnel Hill Trail	166
Sugar Grove	②	Virgil Gilman Trail	171
Sumner	②	Red Hills State Park	142
Sycamore	③	DeKalb-Sycamore Trail	177
Sycamore	③	Great Western Trail	73
Sycamore	③	Peace Road Trail	129
Tampico	①	Hennepin Canal Parkway	80
Taylorville	④	Lincoln Prairie Trail	108
Tinley Park	④	Tinley Creek Forest Preserve	165
Toulon	②	Rock Island State Trail	150
Troy	③	Goshen Trail	31
Troy	③	Schoolhouse Trail	32
Tunnel Hill	①	Tunnel Hill Trail	166
Union	①	HUM Trail	178
Urbana	④	Lake of the Woods FP	106
Vernon Hills	④	Des Plaines River Trail & Greenway	56

City to Trail Index (continued)

County to Trail Index

County to Trail Index (continued)

Illinois Bicycle Related Laws

625 ILCS 5/11-1502 TRAFFIC LAWS APPLY TO PERSONS RIDING BICYCLES
Every person riding a bicycle upon a highway shall be granted all of the rights
and shall be subject to all of the duties applicable to the driver of a vehicle.

625 ILCS 5/11-1503 RIDING ON BICYCLES
    (a) A person propelling a bicycle shall not ride other than upon or
        astride a permanent and regular seat attached thereto.
    (b) No bicycle shall be used to carry more persons at one time than
        the number for which it is designed and equipped, except that an
        adult rider may carry a child securely attached to his person in a
        back pack or sling.

625 ILCS 5/11-1504 CLINGING TO VEHICLES
No person riding upon any bicycle, coaster, roller skates, sled or toy vehicle shall
attach the same or himself to any vehicle upon a roadway.

625 ILCS 5/11-1505 RIDING BICYCLES UPON ROADWAY
Persons riding bicycles upon a roadway shall not ride more than 2 abreast,
except on paths or parts of the roadway set aside for their exclusive use. Persons
riding 2 abreast shall not impede the normal and reasonable movement of traffic
and, on a laned roadway, shall ride within a single lane subject to the provisions
of Section 11-1505 (625 ILCS 5/11-1505).

625 ILCS 5/11-1506 CARRYING ARTICLES
No person operating a bicycle shall carry any package, bundle or article which
prevents the use of both hands in the control and operation of the bicycle. A
person operating a bicycle shall keep at least one hand on the handlebars at all
times.

625 ILCS 5/11-1507 LAMPS AND OTHER EQUIPMENT ON BICYCLES
    (a) Every bicycle, when in use at night time, shall be equipped with a
        lamp on the front, which shall emit white light visible from a distance
        of at least 500 feet to the front and with a red reflector on the rear, of
        a type approved by the Department, which shall be visible from all
        distances from 100 feet to 600 feet to the rear when directly in front
        of lawful lower beams of headlamps on a motor vehicle. A lamp
        emitting a red light visible from a distance of 500 feet to the rear
        may be used in addition to the red reflector.
    (b) A bicycle shall not be equipped with nor shall any person use
        upon a bicycle any siren.
    (c) Every bicycle shall be equipped with a brake which will
        adequately control movement of an stop and hold such bicycle.

625 ILCS 5/11-1509
A uniformed police officer may at any time upon reasonable cause to believe that
a bicycle is unsafe or not equipped as required by law, or that its equipment is not
in proper adjustment or repair, require the person riding the bicycle to stop and
submit the bicycle to an inspection and such text with reference thereto as may
be appropriate.

American Bike Trails publishes and distributes
maps, books and guides for the bicyclist.

For more information:
www.abtrails.com